A Guide to the Maintenance, Repair, and Alteration of Historic Buildings

A Guide to the Maintenance, Repair, and Alteration of Historic Buildings

Frederick A. Stahl

VNR VAN NOSTRAND REINHOLD COMPANY
——————————————————————— New York

Printed in the United States of America

Van Nostrand Reinhold Company Inc.
135 West 50th Street
New York, New York 10020

Van Nostrand Reinhold Company Limited
Molly Millars Lane
Wokingham, Berkshire RG11 2PY, England

Van Nostrand Reinhold
480 La Trobe Street
Melbourne, Victoria 3000, Australia

Macmillan of Canada
Division of Canada Publishing Corporation
164 Commander Boulevard
Agincourt, Ontario M1S 3C7, Canada

16 15 14 13 12 11 10 9 8 7 6 5 4 3 2

Library of Congress Cataloging in Publication Data

Stahl, Frederick A., 1930-
  A guide to the maintenance, repair, and alteration of historic buildings.

  Includes index.
1. Historic buildings—United States—Conservation and restoration.
2. Historic buildings—United States—Maintenance and repair. I. Title.
NA106.S73   1984   720'.28'80973   84-5280
ISBN 0-442-28105-6

CONTENTS

ILLUSTRATIONS

TABLES

There are two purposes of this Guide. One is to help in establishing a continuing program of building care which preserves the physical integrity and visual character of significant GSA properties; the other is to assist in adapting these buildings to contemporary safety, utility, and convenience standards without disturbing their original architectural character.

The Guide addresses only the most common problems of deterioration or failure of building materials and systems found in the majority of GSA's historic buildings; the Guide cannot be the total resource for issues related to the care of these properties.

REGIONAL HISTORIC PRESERVATION OFFICER (RHPO)

There is a Regional Historic Preservation Officer (RHPO) in each region. Building Managers and Regional Designers are strongly urged to consult these persons frequently regarding **any** maintenance, alteration or repair of an historic building, before the work is begun.

ARCHITECTURAL PERIODS

For the purposes of this Guide, Federal construction has been divided into these four major periods:

Early 19th Century and before (1750-1859)
Late 19th Century (1860-1899)
Early 20th Century (1900-1929)
Mid-20th Century (1930-   )

KEY TERMS

Understanding the approach to care addressed by this Guide requires distinguishing among these key terms (other terms frequently used in this Guide are defined in the Glossary):

Preservation. The application of measures designed to maintain the original form, materials and finishes of a structure in an existing physical state by stabilizing the process of deterioration, without major rebuilding, while ensuring the continued safety and habitability of the structure.

Restoration. The application of measures to identify and recover or replace the original forms, materials, finishes, and decoration of a space or structure.

Custodial Care. Regular and periodic cleaning of building surfaces to remove stains, dirt, and foreign material with the mildest methods and materials that prove effective.

Proper custodial care counters the forces that cause deterioration of the building fabric, such as: erosion and abrasion; chemical deterioration; corrosion and mold; and the effects of the most unpredictable factor in building care, human behavior.

Buildings require cleaning because weathering and human activity deposit potentially harmful particles on surfaces. Dirt particles abet abrasion and are often a factor in chemical deterioration processes. Occasionally, special techniques are required to counteract the electrostatic attraction between dirt and certain surfaces, or to arrest or reverse various ongoing chemical changes caused by dirt on sensitive materials.

In historic buildings, where the materials are older, less resistant to abrasive and chemical action than their contemporary counterparts, and frequently irreplaceable, special consideration of the following custodial guidelines is warranted:

1. Understand the nature of both the dirt and the surface to be cleaned before proceeding. Dry cleaning processes (e.g., dusting, polishing, vacuuming, etc.) will remove over half of the dirt; usually at little risk to the structure; wet cleaning (e.g., mopping, washing, etc.) including the use of soaps, detergents, polishes and other compounds to suspend and emulsify dirt particles, are necessary to clean the other half.

2. Use the mildest workable method and cleaning solution in each instance; this may require more time or effort.

3. Refer to historical precedents regarding how the materials have been cared for before choosing a new custodial process.

4. Research and test the suitability of new products before permitting their widespread use on an historic building. Seek the experiences of others before proceeding. Begin work in the less sensitive, less valuable areas of the structure.

5. Remember that decisions involving the care of historic buildings frequently involve "the lesser of two evils;" in some instances, historic materials that might be damaged by repeated cleaning may be better preserved if they remain dirtier than custodial standards would otherwise permit.

6. Clean **only** when a useful purpose is served; don't clean historic materials simply because they are old.

In general, the standard custodial practices of the General Services Administration (refer to GSA Custodial Management Handbook, PBS P 5810.2A) are well suited to the normal demands of interior cleaning in historic buildings, and most exterior cleaning problems as well (e.g., cleaning of glass, architectural metals, etc.; consult Part 3 of the Guide for the special case of masonry cleaning).

The procedures and policies of the General Services Administration regarding the maintenance and repair of conventional buildings (refer to HB, Building Maintenance Management, PBS P 5850.1A) are also applicable to GSA's historic buildings although some changes in emphasis are frequently necessary.

Because a range of alternatives must be considered when confronting any maintenance or repair problem, the following questions are useful:

1. Has the problem and its remedy been identified or only the symptom?

2. Are the resources available to solve the problem on a long-term basis?

3. If not, are visually and technically acceptable interim alternatives available?

4. What are the implications of taking no action or delaying action until a better solution or additional resources are at hand?

5. Does the contemplated maintenance or repair action involve an irreversible effect or destruction of significant fabric? Is the projected benefit worth the risk?

6. Can the situation which caused the problem be remedied by changing the cause rather than treating its result (e.g., reducing the load to eliminate the overstress; changing the use pattern to diminish wear and tear, etc.)?

7. What can be learned from maintenance or repair records about previous attempts to solve the problem? Have other GSA personnel confronted comparable problems in similar buildings?

GRAFFITI

Removal of aerosol paints, crayon, felt-tip marker ink and lipstick is costly and time-consuming. Extensive studies of graffiti-resistant coatings and removal techniques on various building surfaces (National Bureau of Standards Publication No. NBSIR 75-789) reveal that removal by mechanical abrasion with suitable cleaning solvents is most effective, and that a variety of surface coatings (e.g., urethanes, acrylics, silicones) are moderately effective in rejecting the markings.

However, these studies did not evaluate the effect of such techniques and coatings on the fabric itself. Consideration of this issue is essential.

IN GENERAL THE USE OF ANTI-GRAFFITI COATINGS ON HISTORIC BUILDINGS SHOULD BE AVOIDED BECAUSE THEY FREQUENTLY ALTER THE APPEARANCE OF THE COATED SURFACE AND, IN FACT, MAY SERVE AS A PRIMER FOR SOME MARKERS.

BIRDS

Bird droppings on ledges, ornamental detail and roof appurtenances are visually obnoxious, and being acidic, may foster deterioration. Removal of the droppings is discussed under Masonry Cleaning (Section 3.1.4).

"Bird-proofing" alternatives are more complex and costly. They include:

Mechanical Devices: a) Wire mesh covering ledges and detail to discourage roosting is usually unsightly and is to be avoided except as an interim step (well galvanized mesh must be used to avoid rust run-off); b) "pigeon prongs," small brushlike wire devices of stainless steel are also visually intrusive but can be readily affixed to the structure with mastic. The use of mechanical devices which penetrate the fabric of the building is not an acceptable fastening technique.

Electronic Devices: A variety of electronic devices create electromagnetic fields or hot surfaces which repel birds; they require extensive wiring on or beneath surface ledges, frequently cause spalling or chipping during freeze-thaw periods, and are therefore not recommended.

Chemicals: Chemicals are available, usually in pellet form, to eliminate, sterilize or discourage birds. Some solutions may be painted on ledges to discourage roosting; the environmental consequences, as well as the cost and longevity, of all such treatments must be reviewed on a case-by-case basis. Chemicals should be used carefully, and only with proper test documentation and professional advice.

The term "fine art" is usually reserved for artistic works which are at least partially independent in concept and execution from their architectural surroundings. The term "decorative art" describes the artistic embellishment of architecture.

Following are the principal sub-categories established for these two artistic forms:

Fine Art	**Decorative Art**	
Graphics	Ceilings	Metalwork
Drawings	Columns	Mirrors
Murals	Doors and Frames	Mosaic
Painting	Floors	Paneling
Photographs	Fountains	Pilasters
Sculpture (both free-standing and relief)	Furniture	Staircases
	Gates & Gateposts	Walls
Sculpture Bases	Mantels	Windows

Several guidelines should be kept in mind whenever building fabric which might prove to be of artistic importance is encountered:

1. Do not remove or disturb the art in any way unless so required by considerations of security, safety or in an emergency.

2. Do not change the environmental conditions (e.g., temperature, humidity, lighting, etc.), unless a compelling reason exists to do so.

3. Document it (e.g., photograph, sketch, etc.). Always seek expert assistance to identify the work.

4. Advise your Regional Historic Preservation Officer of the situation; include available documentation in your advisory.

The following guidelines supplement the GSA Custodial Handbook and are pertinent to the custody and maintenance of finish materials* prevalent in historic buildings.

**BRASS AND BRONZE:
UNLACQUERED POLISHED FINISH**

Polish at weekly intervals or as required: apply a commercial metal cleaner or polish with a clean, soft cloth, rubbing with the grain of the metal. To avoid staining, apply the cleaner to a limited area and remove quickly by buffing with a clean, soft cloth. A pointed orangewood stick may prove helpful in removing excess polish from crevices and corners. Should staining occur, remove the stain with additional applications of the cleaner.

A suitable clean is

> McIntyre Metal Cleaner
> McIntyre Metal Maintenance
> 1615 South Broadway
> Los Angeles, California 95351
> (213)749-4621

**BRASS AND BRONZE:
LACQUERED POLISHED FINISH**

Remove all old lacquer by applying a stripper of flush-away type methylene chloride with a steel or brass wire brush. Steel wool should not be used to apply the lacquer remover since it is often treated with corrosion inhibitors capable of staining copper base alloys. All strokes of the brush should be with the grain of the metal.

Allow the stripper to stand on the lacquer for several minutes and then remove it by wiping with "clean waste" or by flushing with water. Several applications of the stripper may be necessary to remove all traces of the lacquer.

Follow the stripping operation with an application of metal cleaner, applied with a soft, clean cloth to small areas with the grain of the metal. Immediately remove the cleaner by buffing with a clean, soft cloth. (Recommended cleaners are listed with unlacquered surfaces).

Persistent stains or corrosion may be removed by abrading the surface with Scotch-Brite pads or with pumice and solvent.

Metal surfaces that have undergone dezincification—indicated by pink stains—may be restored by swabbing with a solution containing 5 per cent oxalic acid dissolved in a mixture of three parts water and one part butyl cellosolve. Remove all traces of the acid solution by repeated washing with clean water and wipe dry with a soft cloth.

Remove all cleaner residue by washing at least twice with a standard solvent. Follow by a final wipe with a dryer-greaser.

*for additional information on individual materials, consult Part 3.

The application of clear organic films must follow the cleaning operations within four hours. For best results, two full spray coats of the organic material should be applied. **Do not brush on coatings.**

Suitable products are:

1. Lacquer removers—strippers of methylene chloride type

2. Standard solvent—mixture of 75 per cent toluene, 24 per cent acetone, 1 per cent butyl acetate

3. Dryer-degreaser—butyl cellosolve; trichlor-ethylene

4. Clear coatings—acrylic type, either thermosetting or air dry

(B44 or AT50)	Rohm & Haas Indepence Mall West Philadelphia, PA 19105 (215)592-3000
(Incralac)	Stan Chemical Co. 401 Berlin Street East Berlin, CT 06023 (203)828-0571

STATUARY FINISHES (EXTERIOR)

All metal surfaces colored to statuary brown shades should be maintained by periodic oiling. Apply the oil with a clean, soft cloth. On irregular surfaces, a soft fiber brush applicator may be helpful. The cloths used to apply oil should be retained for reuse and discarded only when they wear out.

Entrance doors and other areas of heavy traffic should be oiled at least every two weeks and fingerprints should be removed daily by wiping lightly with the oiled cloths.

Newly installed metal should be oiled at weekly intervals for approximately one month to build up a protective film.

Entrance frames, trim, and similar light traffic areas should be oiled every few months, as should exterior window frames and curtain wall assemblies. If this frequency is not possible, they should be oiled regularly with intermittent wiping with a soft, dry cloth to remove dust and dirt. Oiling may be combined with window washing procedures.

STATUARY FINISHES (INTERIOR)

All interior statuary finishes in areas of moderate to heavy traffic should be oiled every two weeks; in areas of light traffic, they should be oiled monthly. Fingerprints should be removed daily.

Suitable cleaning materials (with suppliers) are:

1. Lemon oil—5 oz./gallon of parrafin oil (high grade distillate, 100 second viscosity, containing naphthenes, but free of cracked stock such as kerosene Topaz B)

2. Lemon grass oil

   (lemon oils)

   E.H. Sargent & Co.
   7300 N. Linden Avenue
   Chicago, IL 60077
   (312)677-0600

   Crompton & Knowles, Inc.
   1701 Nevens Road
   Fairlawn, NJ 07410
   (201)791-7100

   (paraffin)

   ARCO (Atlantic Richfield Co.)
   Chemical Division
   1500 Market Street
   P.O. Box 7258
   Philadelphia, PA 19101
   (800)523-4420

IRON AND WROUGHT IRON

Painted iron surfaces that are either flaked, chipped, abraded, or inappropriately finished in a high-gloss coating should be refinished as follows:

Using either a paste or semi-paste commercial paint and lacquer remover, brush and No. 000 steel wool, completely remove all of the existing coating. Wash bare metal surfaces with a cloth soaked in mineral spirits to remove all residue left by the remover, and permit the surfaces to dry. Using a short fiber bristle (½ to ¾ inch long) brush, dry-scrub surfaces to remove all loose matter.

Brush-apply one coat of interior alkyd-based metal primer to all surfaces and permit to dry. Brush-apply two coats of alkyd egg-shell enamel in appropriate color. (Generally, cast iron and wrought iron work was originally finished in black or brown/black).

SHEET STEEL AND OTHER PAINTED FERROUS METAL

If surface conditions are similar to those described for wrought iron and cast metal work, follow those procedures, using a high quality alkyd semi-gloss enamel, if desired, in lieu of an eggshell finish.

If surfaces are sound and require only repainting, wash them with a cloth soaked in mineral spirits and wipe dry. If existing paint is a high gloss, brush all surfaces with a high quality softening agent (liquid sandpaper) to provide proper "tooth" for new finish coat. Brush-apply one or two coats, as required, of alkyd egg-shell or semi-gloss enamel.

REFINISHING INTERIOR PAINTED
WOOD

Use the following procedure to obtain a transparent finish:

Using either a paste or semi-paste commercial paint and lacquer remover, brush, and No. 000 steel wool, completely remove the existing coating. Wash woodwork with a cloth soaked in mineral spirits to remove all residue left by the remover and permit to dry. Dry-scrub all corners and ornamental wood to insure complete removal of all loose matter, using a short fiber brush. Check all corners and crevices after the wood has dried for remaining sediment or paint which was not reached by the remover. Using a putty knife or broad knife, carefully remove the matter, and dry-brush the wood clean.

Select an isolated portion of the wood area to apply finish samples.

To an area, approximately 12 inches square, brush apply one coat of oil stain or universal stain in a selected tone. (Note: If the wood originally was stained, as indicated after the removal of paint, match the existing stain as closely as possible. If the wood was not stained, select a stain from the light tonal ranges.)

Depending on wood specie and porosity, permit the new stain to penetrate for a period of five to ten minutes after applying. Wipe all surfaces with a clean, lint-free cloth (cheesecloth or gauze), removing all excess stain. Turn cloth regularly. Permit stain to fully dry (a minimum of 12 hours) before proceeding.

Brush-apply one coat of alkyd or urethane-base satin varnish. This coat should be thin, but not watery. Permit varnish to dry a minimum of 24 hours before proceeding.

After the first coat of varnish has dried, buff the surface with No. 00 steel wool and dry-brush to remove all metal particles. Apply a second full-strength coat of satin varnish and permit to fully dry.

When the second coat of varnish has dried, buff with No. 00 steel wool and dry-brush clean. (Note: If second coat is to be final coat, use No. 000 steel wool.)

Depending on the wood's porosity, a third coat of varnish may be required. If so, follow procedures for second coat and buff with No. 000 steel wool.

After the sample has been approved, follow the same procedures for remaining wood.

(Note: On open grain wood species, such as oak, a toned paste filler may be desired before staining. If so, apply a high-quality paste wood filler to surface, and wipe it off across the grain so that the filler remains in the grain depressions. Use a mineral spirits-dampened cloth for wiping. Permit the filler to fully dry before staining.)

For areas subject to wear, such as handrails, wainscots, and the like, apply one coat of non-yellowing paste wax after buffing the final coat of varnish, and buff the wax to a uniform sheen with a lamb's wool pad.

REFINISHING INTERIOR WOODWORK

These guidelines are for transparent finished, non-traffic surfaces having numerous coatings of darkened varnish and/or shellac or surfaces which are worn, abraded, chipped, or otherwise deteriorated.

Following the previous instructions for painted woodwork, strip existing finish to bare wood. After stripping, if the existing wood tone is desired, proceed with finishing. Otherwise, apply stain and finish.

REFINISHING INTERIOR WOOD FLOORING AND OTHER TRAFFIC SURFACES

For painted, varnished, or shellacked surfaces, strip existing finishes to bare wood. Use either a high quality remover and methods previously specified for painted woodwork, or strip by manual or power sanding, using a medium grit paper for the initial passes and then a fine grit for the final passes.

Caution: In sanding, be careful not to erode historic flooring, or to expose nails or splines; generally, chemical removers only should be used. (See Section 3.7 for more information on removing old finishes.)

Completely remove all sanding dust by sweeping, vacuuming, and finally, dry-mopping or wiping with a lint-free dry cloth. After the wood has been stripped but not yet filled, bleach out any surface stains with a wood bleach manufactured for the purpose. Mix and apply the bleach according to the manufacturer's recommendations.

For open grain wood, such as oak, a paste wood filler is recommended to prevent dirt from lodging in the pores. Apply as previously specified for painted wood.

After stripping, if the wood does not need further staining, proceed with finishing; otherwise, apply stain in the manner specified for painted wood.

After the wood, stained or unstained, is completely dry, apply one coat of clear, penetrating-type, alkyd-base or urethane-base floor sealer. Use two coats for soft-wood surfaces. After each coat of sealer is completely dry, lightly sand the surfaces in the direction of the grain, using extra fine grit paper.

Thoroughly clean the sealed surfaces by vacuum and dry-mopping to remove all sanding dust. Apply two coats of alkyd-base or urethane-base floor varnish, gloss or semi-gloss (satin) as desired. (Note: Use only a varnish type compatible with the type of sealer used.)

Lightly sand the first coat of varnish when it is completely dry, using extra fine grit paper. Burnish the second coat of

9

varnish when it is completely dry, using No. 000 steel wool and a floor buffing machine. After burnishing, vacuum and dry mop all surfaces to remove remaining steel wood particles.

Apply one coat of non-yellowing paste wax and mechanically buff to a uniform sheen.

REFINISHING INTERIOR MARBLE

Marble that has been treated with surface coatings requiring removal should be refinished as follows:

Apply a liquid or paste lacquer and paint remover to the surface. Let the remover set until coating has softened, and remove the finish with clean, unsaturated cloths only. Repeat the remover application and removal procedures until the finishes have been completely removed.

Then scrub the surface with a mild detergent powder and fiber brush, and rinse with clear water. Permit the surfaces to fully dry.

Bleach any color pigmentation remaining on the marble surface with a peroxide poultice or a poultice of liquid solvent cleaner manufactured specifically for cleaning and bleaching of marble, following all procedures recommended by the manufacturer.

Caution: Under no circumstances should acids, abrasives, or metal tools be used in cleaning or stripping marblework, except as specifically set forth herein. Acids and some alkalines will dull marble and will leave surfaces vulnerable to yellowing as well as dirt and fungus deposits. Abrasives will likely leave scars and scratches which cannot be removed. Most metal tools, even with careful usage, can scratch or gouge marble surfaces. If a large broadknife would be helpful in removing paint, use a plastic broadknife.

After marble has been completely stripped, cleaned, bleached, rinsed, and fully dried, apply one or two coats of clear penetrating sealer, manufactured by or approved by a reputable marble producer, in strict accordance with the manufacturer's recommendations.

REPAIRING SCRATCHED STONE

For stone that is scratched and/or requires refinishing, mix and apply a liquid cleaner, manufactured specifically for the purpose, in strict accordance with the manufacturer's recommendations. Rinse the cleaned surfaces with clear water and permit to dry.

Obtain a polishing kit for granite or marble, as applicable, from a marble or granite producer, and follow all scratch-removing and polishing procedures.

Caution: Do not use any material or perform any operation on polished granite or marble surfaces not specifically recommended by the respective stone producers.

WOOD AND FURNITURE OILS AND POLISHES

Marquetry should be kept from drying out by occasional rubbing with oil-based furniture polish; for especially delicate objects, almond oil may be required. Furniture with a good polished surface should be rubbed with a soft cloth at regular intervals. The original polish should be preserved, if possible, because it improves with age. Furniture polish is desirable because it coats the surface with a thin wax film, but it should not be allowed to collect in the cracks or crevices where it will attract dirt and detract from appearance. A cleaning emulsion should be made by vigorously shaking together half a pint each of linseed oil, turpentine, and vinegar with a teaspoon of methylated spirit. This emulsion is inexpensive, removes dirt, polishes, and is harmless if it is applied in moderation and the excess removed.

FOR ADDITIONAL HELP OR GUIDANCE IN MAINTAINING INTERIOR FINISHES, CONSULT YOUR REGIONAL HISTORIC PRESERVATION OFFICER (RHPO).

Standard alteration techniques and solutions often will not preserve the architectural character of significant interiors. In general, alterations to such spaces should conceal necessary work, particularly electrical and mechanical equipment, behind the original finishes and within the original structure of the building.

The following design considerations will be helpful.

DESIGN CONSIDERATIONS

Preserve all original finishes, trim and ornament of the room, and remove any existing later alterations or non-original elements.

Repair or replace any missing original features to exact original design and appearance, budget permitting.

Ensure that custodial work and routine maintenance are carried out with utmost care and with only mild, dilute chemical cleaners, if any.

Locate tenants in appropriate spaces. Organize heavy traffic to avoid damaging sensitive areas.

Do not crowd rooms with furnishings that cover architectural detail.

Carefully design and place any necessary electrical outlets or HVAC grilles to be unobtrusive, and paint them to match adjacent finishes.

Remove fluorescent lighting and use concealed uplighting for general illumination and individual task lights at work surfaces. Restore original fixtures, if possible, for general illumination.

Alterations should be compatible with the original space and materials. Use materials and installations that are visually related to finishes and materials in the remainder of the building.

Permit only changes or alterations to materials or finishes necessary for restoration.

Investigate opportunities to conceal all electrical and mechanical equipment when budget permits. Exposed installations of mechanical systems must be laid out as unobtrusively as possible, and should not cover or obscure original elements.

Do not make alterations that attach permanently to original elements of the room. When it is necessary to cover or obscure original elements with alterations, alterations should be easily removable without damage to permanent finishes.

Retain original blinds whenever possible. If an accurate restoration of sun control devices is infeasible, use an unobtrusive contemporary treatment (e.g., thin-line, horizontal blinds). **Do not:** paint over window glass; change clear glass to frosted or translucent glass; replace glass with solid filler panel; use vertical blinds or wall-to-wall drapery; cover decorative window surrounds with shades or blinds; use roller shades.

Test ceiling for original colors and details and restore to exact original condition.

Preserve, maintain and repair and match flooring where possible. If intensive use is damaging the flooring, install high quality carpeting or new protective coatings, but do not use adhesives or tacks in a way that will damage original floor.

CONTACT YOUR REGIONAL HISTORIC PRESERVATION OFFICER (RHPO) FOR FURTHER GUIDANCE.

The following areas of planning and design afford the designer an opportunity to maintain proper preservation design standards when altering significant interiors.

SPACE MANAGEMENT: FIT THE SPACE TO THE TENANT

The proper fit between tenant and space can reduce the extent of alterations needed. When assigning space, consider these general procedures:

1. Carefully evaluate the existing building to determine its condition, capacity, and reuse potential; assess and categorize the relative importance of all spaces.

2. Prepare a program that clearly states the technical and spatial requirements of the tenant.

3. Strive for compatibility between the tenant and the space. For example, do not assign a highly detailed space to a user requiring installation of special mechanical systems which would compromise the special character of the space. Similarly, do not assign large, well-detailed rooms to an office user requesting a high proportion of small, private offices.

FIND NEW SPACE IN UNUSED SPACE

Many larger nineteenth and twentieth century buildings contain extremely large attic and basement spaces intended only for storage, and large corridors which constitute a much higher percentage of the usable space than is required today. By supplying power, lighting, HVAC, toilets, and necessary insulation and finishes to such spaces, the net usable square footage within a building can be greatly increased for less than the cost of new construction. The insulation of such spaces, particularly attics, will reduce the heat loss through the roof, thereby reducing the operating cost.

Often these spaces have open wood or metal trusses that accommodate open office plan layouts. The open truss work is an architectural feature that may be preserved intact, without being covered with fireproofing, where sprinkler systems are installed or planned. Sprinklers can be extended simply and relatively inexpensively to an attic to provide fire protection.

RECOMMENDED PARTITIONING PRACTICES

Some relatively new concepts and devices for rearranging space are available to the interior designer faced with resolving tenant needs without compromising preservation standards.

1. **Partial Height, Movable Partitions:** Partial height partitions can effectively form satisfactory semi-private and private offices, and conference rooms within the large, high-ceilinged rooms found in many of GSA's historic buildings. Because they are often free-standing, architectural trim and details do

not have to be disturbed or interrupted.

2. **Furniture:** Certain furniture elements can be used as space dividers in open plan layouts. It is not necessary, for example, to place file cabinets, storage units, and book shelves against the walls, obscuring architectural features such as wainscoting or carved baseboards. Rather, these units (if coordinated) can be used together as partial enclosures for offices and work spaces. These furnishings may be painted to match the space's color scheme.

DISCOURAGED PARTITIONING PRACTICES

Full-height partitions are discouraged.

Most prefabricated, full-height partitions are designed to be incorporated into a full system, including a suspended ceiling grid. While contemporary office spaces created from these prefabricated systems appear neat, clean and efficient they are generally out of character in an historic building. Moreover, the structural framework of an historic building may not readily accommodate such systems without considerable alteration and cost.

Therefore, these systems should be avoided, except in space of little architectural character. Should a full-height partition system be required, minimize its visibility from major public sidewalks or streets, public spaces, lobbies or corridors.

Some other specific space planning precautions concern the following:

1. **Structural Walls:** Alterations to structural walls are complex and expensive and **should be avoided whenever possible.** Disturbing an historic building's structure can cause cracks in plaster or in flooring, among other problems.

2. **Non-structural Walls:** Such alterations should be undertaken only when necessary, using the following guides: a) Do not alter existing partitions in important, significant space; b) Permit only minimal alterations to existing partitions in moderately important spaces; and c) Permit alterations as necessary in spaces of minimal architectural character.

3. **Doorways:** If an original doorway is no longer to be used, the door should be locked and left undisturbed. Do not remove it. New doorways should not be cut into important spaces. New doorways should be treated as simply and as unobtrusively as possible, or should be matched exactly to the original treatment of the existing doors, including paneling and trim.

Creativity and innovation are necessary ingredients to agreeable solutions.

CONSULT YOUR REGIONAL HISTORIC PRESERVATION OFFICER ON SPACE REORGANIZATION PROBLEMS.

FIGURE 2.2.1
INTERIOR SPACE RENOVATION GUIDELINES

PERSPECTIVES

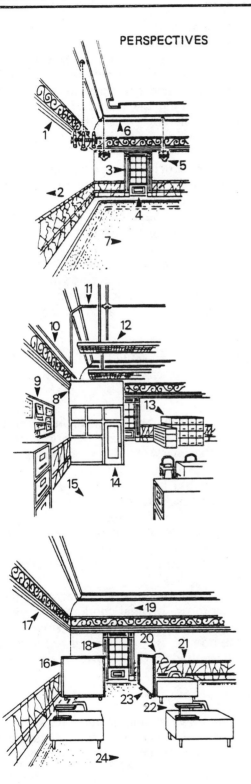

ORIGINAL CONDITIONS

1. Cornice or Frieze
2. Wainscot
3. Window Trim
4. Decorative Panel
5. Lighting Fixture
6. Ceiling Moldings and Enrichment
7. Wood or Stone Finish Floor

EXISTING CONDITIONS

8. Non-structural partition butted into architectural trim
9. General visual clutter
10. Surface applied raceway running in view along original trim
11. Surface applied raceway running across original trim
12. Suspended fluorescent fixtures interfere with perception of space and architectural detail; create glare
13. Office furniture carelessly arranged so as to obscure architectural detail
14. High non-structural partition assemblies alter character of space and impose incongruous materials
15. Wall-to-wall carpeting or resilient flooring

PROPOSED MEASURES TO RE-EMPHASIZE ORIGINAL CHARACTER OF SPACE BY MINIMIZING INTRUSIONS

16. High non-structural partition replaced by portable screen (possibly incorporating sound absorbing or other special characteristics) which does not interfere with continuity of original elements.
17. Original architectural elements exposed by removing intrusive elements.
18. See 17.
19. Removal of suspended fluorescent fixtures and surface raceways reduces visual clutter.
20. New task lighting compensates for loss of general illumination.
21. Removal of furniture from perimeter of room exposes original trim and adds to apparent size of room.
22. See 20.
23. Portable partitions enclose private office while permitting better perception of entire space and can create amenities such as more space (possibly shared) and better light.
24. Removal of carpet or resilient flooring to expose original finish floor.

Matching architectural materials and design details is important in repair, renovation and restoration.

GSA's significant buildings are generally quite well documented and necessary information may be obtained from available drawings, records, and correspondence. In addition, information is readily available concerning the works of many of the architects responsible for notable government buildings; it may be possible to extrapolate from one work sufficient detail about another.

Caution: In instances where conclusive documentation is unavailable, dates must be established by stylistic analysis, a process requiring an architectural historian or an industrial archeologist, and frequently entailing extensive research. It is therefore not covered in this Guide and is not a recommended procedure for GSA personnel lacking such special training.

The largest problem for the project manager is obtaining competent craftsmen to properly reproduce period workmanship at an affordable price. The Regional Historic Preservation Officer can assist in searching for such qualified craftsmen and contractors.

LIGHTING

Where original chandeliers still exist or will be fabricated from original drawings, indirect lighting can be concealed within the chandelier.

If original drawings are not available, photographs of original fixtures often can be found in local or state historical society files, architectural libraries, National Archives, or newspaper files. If the intended restoration is of public interest, a drawing or photograph of the fixture should be published in a local newspaper with a request for information about similar fixtures. An actual fixture to copy can sometimes be obtained in this manner. Accurate reproduction, particularly where new patterns must be carved, is essential. Good existing reproductions of period fixtures are not available today for the majority of the fixtures used in GSA's historic buildings.

Conduit should not normally be run exposed across ceilings or walls; it is often possible to use original conduit for rewiring. Though difficult, wire usually can be fished behind wood paneling, old plaster walls, baseboards, etc., with much less patching and repair than would be required to cut grooves or channels in plaster surfaces.

DORMERS

Dormers should be inspected carefully each time the roof is inspected. Maintenance of dormers should include repair or replacement of siding material, roof material, shape and structure, window and window operation, trim and molding. In many buildings, dormers provide a basis for determining original exterior paint colors because they have been painted less frequently than other parts of the exterior.

WINDOWS, FRAMES, SASH, AND SUN CONTROL

Repairs and alterations to windows, frames and sash should be accomplished by in-kind replacement of existing materials. Maintain the appearance of the original members by observing as many of the following criteria as is possible:

1. The frame of the sash and muntins should be the same size and shape as the original and, if possible, the molding profile on the original members should be duplicated.

2. The color and finish of the new frame members should match those of the originals. For this reason, paint color tests should be made on the original sash.

3. Window frames should match the shape of all existing trim and molding. The frames should be treated with wood preservative.

4. If the frames are removed, their size, shape, and molding profiles should be duplicated by the replacements.

5. The operation of the windows should remain the same because changing their operation will alter their appearance. (Casement windows do not look like double-hung windows.)

6. The overall size of the replacement sash and window frames should be the same as the original. Do not fill openings to accommodate smaller standard windows.

7. Use clear glass. Primary reduction of summer sunlight should be by use of interior blinds, which are much more effective than tinted glass, and do not change the exterior appearance of the building. If the appearance of light-colored blinds is a concern, blinds may be selected in a darker color.

Stock sash seldom matches the size and shape of the original window and frame members. All new frame members should match the varying dimensions of original members as well as the configuration of each frame and sash type. When energy conservation measures necessitate double glazing, existing sash members should be rabbeted out to enable the thicker glass to be accommodated; in instances where this is not possible, deeper members of otherwise identical profiles should be milled.

Preservation policy discourages the use of storm windows or

the replacement of original sash without careful analysis of alternatives.

DOORS

Replacement doors should match original doors, even though they may be wood which may require considerable maintenance.

CHIMNEYS

Chimneys in need of rebuilding should be replaced with material and detailing that match the original. The cap and the decorative coursing around it, often in a different material, deserve particularly accurate re-creation.

The same general chimney size should be maintained for the entire building. When upgrading of a boiler plant requires a new chimney for a flue, every effort should be made to carry the new flue up within an existing chimney to avoid changing the exterior character of the building. The flue can be inserted into an existing chimney by cutting into it and joining flue pipes at each floor.

New chimneys should not be run up the exterior face of an existing building. Interior changes for a new chimney are preferable, provided that no significant interior spaces are disturbed. Should it become necessary to construct an exterior chimney, the material used should match or be compatible with the existing original exterior materials.

The most important sources of information on a building include: 1) Original drawings and construction files; 2) Subsequent alteration documents and construction files; and 3) Early photographs of the building.

SOURCES OF INFORMATION

The Regional Historic Preservation Officer should maintain information files on each historic property in the Region, including drawings, photographs, specifications, shop drawings, correspondence, and relevant information on the style and design characteristics of the period of construction. Other sources of information may be found in:

The Building

Often sets or partial sets of both original and subsequent alteration documents are stored away and forgotten in an attic closet, or an old fileroom.

National Archives and Records Service (NARS)

Documentation on historic Federal buildings is available at NARS. Copies of any material found locally which does not exist in the National Archives should be forwarded to NARS.

Local and State Historical Societies

Additional documentation is often available through libraries and film archives maintained by local and state historical societies; early photographs in particular, both exterior and interior, may show original materials and detailing destroyed by subsequent alteration. Both state and private historical organizations, including the local chapter of the American Institute of Architects and the State Historic Preservation Officer, should be contacted.

Local and Major State Newspapers

Local and major state newspapers published at the time the building was designed and constructed, altered, or enlarged may contain photographs or descriptions that will identify unknown items.

Municipal Files

Building Inspection, Planning and Zoning Offices may contain copies of original plans as well as alteration plans.

When the restoration of a particular item or items is planned and exact documentation has not yet been obtained, it is worthwhile to ask the feature editor of the major local newspaper to run an article on the project, requesting any reader with knowledge, photographs, or other documents of historic information on the specific items or on the building in general to make them available to the RHPO for copying. If the original documents are obtained, their source should be recorded.

USE OF ORIGINAL DRAWINGS

Because they are unique and often fragile or in poor condition, original drawings or other source material should not be filed for

21

general use. Wherever possible **reproducible** copies of such material should be made, as well as arrangements for permanent storage of the originals with a local, regional, or national archival facility having proper conditions and trained personnel.

RECORD PHOTOGRAPHY

Photography is one of the most useful documentary tools available today. Every RHPO should have access to basic photographic equipment, and know how to use it. The usual photographic techniques employed are:

Photogrammetry

In certain instances, particularly where a large scale exterior renovation of a major building is being planned in the absence of original drawings, or where a building is simply unrecorded, photogrammetry can be used to produce exact elevations, sections, and even plans, as well as to detect deformation or movement of surfaces and cracking.

X-Ray Photography

The National Park Service and other preservation agencies have used a new portable X-ray generator and film to record subsurface conditions whose examination otherwise would require the destruction of surface materials. Through the use of X-ray photography techniques, it is possible to detect condition details of the structure; the location and sizes of members, including wood framing and nailing, joists, steel columns, beams, and bracing; the location and types of masonry reinforcing and wall ties; and the alignment and plumb, cracking, or other signs of deterioration within the walls, floors, and ceilings.

Infra-Red Photography

Because it indicates variation in temperature levels, infra-red photography is being used to detect material decomposition and deterioration as well as leaks and areas of water infiltration, particularly in exterior wall construction and roofs where sources of leaks are often extremely difficult to detect.

As a result of increasing recognition of alternative modes of compliance available to satisfy the intent of life safety and fire control provisions of Building Regulatory Agencies, (especially as these relate to Historic Buildings), extensive survey, research and development has been undertaken in recent years by such organizations as the Center for Building Technology at the National Bureau of Standards, the National Trust for Historic Preservation, and a number of State regulatory agencies.

As a result of a joint program between the State Building Code Commission of the Commonwealth of Massachusetts and N.B.S., new Code provisions have been adopted as Article 22, and Appendix T of the State Building Code of the Commonwealth of Massachusetts.

These provide for the public safety, health and general welfare by permitting repair or alterations of, additions to, and change of use of existing buildings and structures or parts thereof, without requiring the existing building or structure to comply with all of the requirements of the Code for new construction.

The approach taken applies techniques of acceptable practice which can be used to assess the acceptability of various methods of meeting the intent of the Code provisions with respect to individual buildings on a case by case basis. The system involves an assessment of risk by occupancy type together with the application of alternative acceptable means of risk reduction.

The documents in question may be obtained from:

State Building Code Commission
John W. MacCormack State Office Building
One Ashburton Place
Room 1305
Boston, MA 02108

Common sense and past experience are the best guide to applying energy conservation techniques to older buildings; such buildings were built prior to the invention of sophisticated HVAC systems, and they have qualities which are inherently energy-efficient (e.g., thick walls, minimal glass, plans conceived for natural lighting and ventilation, etc.). In re-using such buildings, the designer is wise to consider these valuable characteristics, and to seek designs that enhance and augment these attributes.

ENERGY RETROFIT PROGRAM

Buildings can be improved as follows:

HVAC Equipment

The replacement of actual mechanical equipment and systems in historic buildings is reviewed in Part 5.

Insulation of Pipes and Ducts

The decision to insulate pipes and ducts often hinges on whether they are exposed or concealed. If the systems are concealed behind original finishes, the additional expense to remove and replace finishes and the disruption of the occupants may not warrant the undertaking.

Weatherstripping

This is an inexpensive and effective way to reduce infiltration losses from windows, doors, skylights, vents, louvers, etc. On a temporary basis, without removal of sash, cracks and loose fitting windows can be weatherstripped with felt, vinyl, or rubber gasket strips. Care in the selection and installation of weatherstripping could, however, permit operation of the sash—preferably the lower sash only—without disturbing the integrity of the seal.

Lighting

New lighting systems are readily compatible with historic preservation concerns, and they should be explored. Evenly spaced, suspended fluorescent lighting is generally inappropriate in significant architectural spaces, and should be removed, along with suspended tile ceilings, if present.

New long-life, low-energy sources should be used to replace fluorescent fixtures. The best color rendition is created by quartz sources which are far more efficient than normal incandescent lighting; other sources, such as metal halide or mercury vapor, are still twice as efficient as a fluorescent source, although the color range is less satisfactory. Exercise care in the choice of both lamp and manufacturer because the technology in this field is just developing and manufacturers have not yet developed uniform luminaire performance.

Wall Insulation

In an existing building, the installation of wall insulation is limited by finishes. In some cases, insulation can be blown into the wall cavity through holes cut into the finish, but the process is ineffective and is not recommended.

New products using a similar technique—blowing insulation into wall cavities with hose and pump—include plastic foams which set up, solidify, and remain permanently in place to provide full protection. Such foams overcome a problem which other post-construction installations do not solve: they provide a vapor barrier, which prevents water from condensing in the insulation material. While not in use long enough to have received time-tested evaluation, such an insulation method is tentatively recommended where heat loss through the walls is a significant problem.

Note: the flammability and toxicity of any foam insulation should be carefully evaluated.

Attic Insulation

Greater heat loss normally occurs through the roof of a building than through the walls. Attic insulation, including a vapor barrier underneath it, should be applied to the attic floor if the attic is unused. Should the attic be converted into habitable space, the insulation should be applied on the underside of the roof framing. Rigid insulation board can also be applied over the roof construction, when a complete replacement of the finish roofing is scheduled. Almost any proven type of insulation can be applied in an accessible attic space.

Ceiling Insulation

There is a common misconception that the installation of a suspended acoustical tile ceiling within an original high-ceilinged space reduces the volume of space to be heated or cooled. Such a ceiling has only a minor effect on the heating or cooling demand, since the space above remains within the overall building volume. Only completely sealing and insulating such a space would significantly impact the total heating or cooling load. There is little need for thermal separation between floors.

Double Glazing

For thermal efficiency, double glazing is recommended where it can be readily accommodated in existing sash or in similar sash.

Necessary alterations in older properties to make them completely accessible to the handicapped can have an adverse impact on the building's appearance. There are no iron-clad rules about the best way to make the necessary accommodations; the appropriate solution will vary from building to building, depending upon its unique features and design. However, some solutions have been used successfully to satisfy the requirements without significantly disturbing architectural character:

MEANS OF ENTRY

In new construction and alteration projects, ramps are required when the first floor is above the grade or sidewalk. However, the size and mass of a ramp can seriously disturb the original design and character of the entrance. Where necessary, a secondary entrance may be chosen to preserve the architectural integrity of prime entrances, and a small sign should be placed at the main entrance, giving the location of the ramp.

If the budget and extent of renovation permit, a small hydraulic elevator at a secondary street level entrance can be installed to serve the main floor, where the main elevators serve the remainder of the building. Often a new grade level entrance can be created in relation to a window or a stair landing, if the stair is against the exterior wall.

INTERIOR LEVEL CHANGES

Where interior level changes prevent access to public facilities either access or comparable facilities elsewhere in the building should be provided. Where level changes prevent access to offices or working spaces, the only alternative may be a ramp within the corridor space. Such installations must not damage or disturb original floor materials.

DOORWAYS

Where doors to necessary facilities are too small for wheelchairs, a useful approach is to remove and reinstall a larger, framed opening with matching trim and finish from a less important location in the building. This avoids the cost and the difficulty of matching original work with new work.

SCHEDULING THE INSPECTION

Periodic inspections are the responsibility of the R&A Branch in each region. Recommended inspection frequencies are shown in the Building Inspection Checklist (Table 2.8.2) as well as the areas to be examined. If time, personnel or budget do not permit these schedules, do not abandon a program of periodic inspection; instead, establish a program based on extended intervals. However, extending inspection intervals beyond three years considerably lessens the first line of defense in budget control.

Inspect exteriors between March and October, when conditions are safest, particularly regarding roofs and upper exterior wall areas and all exterior surfaces exposed to view. Spring and early summer months should be reserved for the most deteriorated buildings because, if the need for emergency or immediate exterior repair is discovered, the balance of summer and fall months will be available for the work before inclement weather begins.

INSPECTION PRIORITIES

Inspections should address issues involving the activities within, or operation of, the building itself, including space utilization, tenant convenience, equipment operation, energy consumption, etc.

An inspection report should be a bias-free record of the condition of the building, any symptoms and potential problems. In this phase, record symptoms observed and causes deduced, not remedies recommended.

PREPARING FOR THE INSPECTION

1. If possible, inspections should always be made by a team of two people, one of whom, the team chief, has engineering qualifications and field experience. The chief's assistant should be in training for inspection duties.

2. Examine one or two of the most recent Inspection Reports. Note items of special concern to be re-examined.

CONDUCTING THE INSPECTION

1. Review the present and anticipated repair and alterations schedule with the BM; check that all items have been reviewed by the BM with RHPO.

2. Review current status of GSA programs as they apply to the particular building(s) under inspection.

3. Establish an orderly progression for the inspection. Although each building may suggest its own order of inspection—which is established by the team chief—this Guide begins with the exterior, from the roof down. (See Building Inspection Checklist, and Figures 2.8.1 and 2.8.2)

27

4. At the end of the inspection, review the field BIR and ensure that all necessary information has been completed and that all special conditions or problems have been noted for the preparation of a file copy.

AFTER THE INSPECTION

1. Prepare a one-page summary of the significant findings and observations made during the inspection.

2. Prepare a file copy of a suitable inspection report from the field copy and notes. A suggested format is:

Building Name and Number

GSA Region

Address

Date

Identity of Reporter(s)

Use and Occupancy

Recent Changes in Use, Occupancy

Description of General Size and Arrangement of Structure

Description of Condition of Structural Materials

Present Complaint

Past Problems (in same area)

Observations of the Specific Problem

Description and Measurements of Surface Conditions (pitching floors, cracking plaster, etc.)

Photographs Taken

Observations of Similar Locations in Surrounding Areas

Measurements Made

Persons Contacted about the Problem

STRUCTURAL INVESTIGATION

Frequently, potential structural problems will be discovered in the course of a regular inspection, either from a complaint or as a result of a proposed change to the building. These problems are best understood and remedied if an orderly sequence of investigation is followed. The recommended sequence for conducting a structural investigation is:

Identify the Sympton

1. Verify the current problem and record it on appropriate form noting the exact signs of distress and where they were reported.

2. Inspect the entire building to determine if the problem exists elsewhere or is limited to a particular area. (For example, if cracks occur on one corner of the structure, check to see if they are repeated on the adjacent or opposing corners.)

3. Inspect for related problems. (For example, determine if there is water damage to the interior plaster in addition to the cracked brickwork.)

4. Record your observations of the problem as well as other pertinent data.

5. Determine if the problem is stable or increasing: a) check records for previous repairs; b) check previous repairs; c) undertake simple measurements (e.g., measure cracks, photograph conditions, etc.); d) undertake elaborate measurements (e.g., precise surveys to determine settlement, technical testing of components, etc.)

6. Determine the general arrangement and the materials of the structural system from: a) old drawings; b) observation of exposed structure (in basement, attic and unfinished spaces, pipe and duct shafts, etc.); c) remove portions of the finish to expose the structure; d) X-ray structure through the finish materials.

7. Refer to Parts 3 and 4 in this Guide for a discussion of problems likely to be encountered in a particular building type, structural system, or construction material.

Determine the Probable Cause of the Problem

1. Select the observed complaint and probable cause from the accompanying Table 2.8.1. Changes in the immediate surroundings of the building can give rise to structural problems. Table 2.8.1 offers a framework for analyzing environmental conditions that might be the cause of structural deficiencies.

2. By observation, narrow down possibilities to the most likely and explore those causes first.

3. Select one or more firms or agencies as necessary to carry out a detailed investigation if: a) it cannot be done in-house; b) the problem appears to be increasing; c) the probable cause is not readily apparent; d) a high priority repair may clearly be required.

ROOF INSPECTION

Both the exterior and the underside of the roof structure should be inspected at close hand; inspection from the ground is virtually useless. In many cases, the first signs of failure will appear on the underside before they are noticeable on the exterior. Use ladders, safety lines and temporary catwalks as necessary for safety, full accessibility, and protection of the finish roofing to conduct a proper inspection of roof surface.

While inspecting the exterior, note any deflection of the roof structure and the condition of the roof pitch, flashing, gutters, roof openings, chimney stacks, parapet walls, coping, and other appurtenances. On the interior, structural deflection or failure can be more closely examined. Any evidence of water stains, condensation, rot, fungi, or insect attack should be noted.

FIGURE 2.8.1
COMMON EXTERIOR PROBLEMS

1. Chimney
2. Flashing
3. Sealant
4. Brick Wall
5. Stone Wall
6. Stucco Wall
7. Wood Trim
8. Shingle (Slate, Tile) Roofs
9. Metal Roofs
10. Bituminous Roofs
11. Gutters and Downspouts

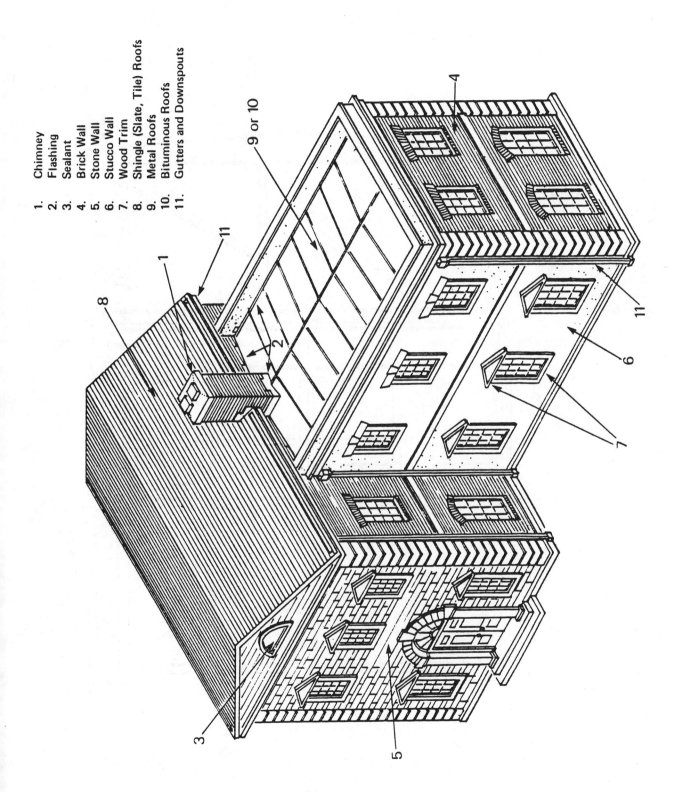

FIGURE 2.8.2
COMMON INTERIOR PROBLEMS

1. Steel Floor Systems
2. Masonry Floor Systems
3. Wood Floor Systems
4. Finish Floor
5. Plaster
6. Interior Steel or Cast Iron Columns
7. Interior Wood Columns
8. Reinforced Concrete
9. Wood Trim
10. Drains & Sewers

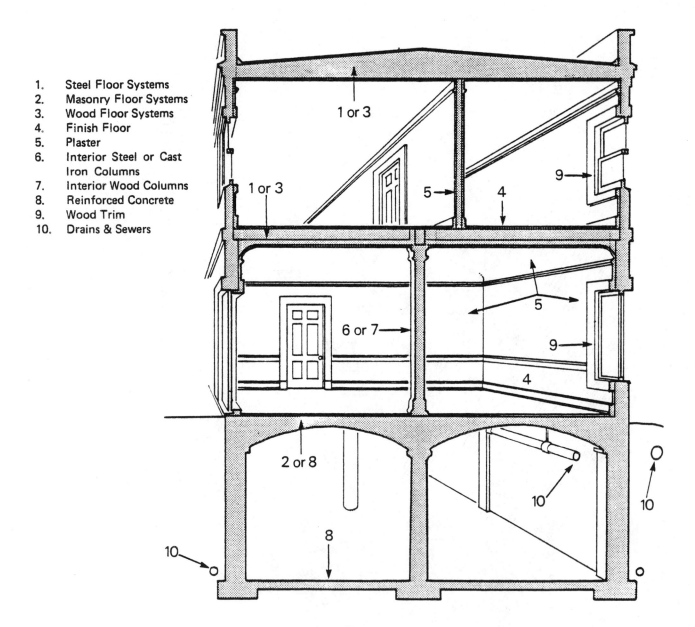

Table 2.8.1
Structural Evaluation After Environmental Change

Exterior Changes:

Factor	Effects	Consequences	Evaluation Techniques
New adjacent construction	Pile driving and blasting	Vibration can cause cracking of plaster & masonry; it may also result in temporary instability of fine sand and silt embankments.	Survey entire building; locate measure & photograph all cracks and other visible distress; establish bench marks on both interior & exterior to monitor movement (both vertical & horizontal).
	Lower water table (usually from continuous pumping from deep foundations).	Decay of untreated exposed wood piles (widely used for sub-grade support prior to 1930).	Establish observation wells to monitor ground water behavior before, during and after adjacent new construction.
		Continuous pumping (often to force water back into surrounding areas) may cause a surcharge which disturbs foundations and causes settlement.	Avoid inducing water so that it alters normal ground water patterns.
	Demolition	Occasional vibration and stray debris.	Survey as provided above.
	Deep excavations	In addition to the hazard of lowered ground water there is a risk of collapse or subsidence from improperly shored and braced excavations.	Professional evaluation and certification is required.
Air Pollution	Airborne pollutants are often introduced into an area by automotive exhaust emissions, nearby industry, or discharge from buildings and energy plants using coal or high sulfur oils.	Airborne pollutants frequently cause soiling and/or deterioration of masonry and metals by combining with water or other present agents to form corrosive chemicals.	Conduct a visual and chemical analysis of surrounding environment and of the building exterior; testing for pH levels, constituent component analysis, etc., may be required.

Table 2.8.1 (continued)

Factor	Effects	Consequences	Evaluation Techniques
Infestation Insects (e.g. termites, powder post beetles, etc.)	Infestation of wood building elements (e.g. structure, trim, etc.). is common in the South and has been gradually increasing in the North.	Deterioration; reduced structural capacity; impaired performance; unsightly appearance.	See Sect. 3.4.

Interior Changes:

Factor	Effects	Consequences	Evaluation Techniques
Heavier floor loads.	Changing functions introduce new demands (e.g. heavy equipment, occupancy of formerly unused space, etc.) and longer use tends to create greater storage needs (e.g. computer cards, back records, etc.); all imply heavier floor loads.	Increasing deflection, cracking of affected finishes; potential overstress.	Investigation and certification by a structural engineer is usually warranted; also consult OSHA standards.
Fire	Direct damage and secondary effects of firefighting operations (e.g. chopping holes, flooding with water, etc.).	Diminished capacity, impaired function; unsightly appearance; lingering odor.	Visual inspection computation; review of fire fighters' records and photographs taken prior to and during a fire.
HVAC	Installation frequently involves cutting secondary wall and floor framing members.	Localized diminished capacity and overstress; can lead to progressive failure.	Whenever possible, subject such renovation plans to prior approval of architect and/or engineer; in all cases, record such work to permit subsequent evaluation; undertake selective removal or X-ray analysis where required to reveal extent of potential damage.
Introduction of air conditioning and humidification	Presence of moisture in unanticipated and previously dry locations (e.g. interior surface of windows and walls, undersides of floors, cooler, etc.).	Possible deterioration due to freeze/thaw cycle, rot, etc.	Visual evaluation, psychrometric measurement and analysis.

Table 2.8.2
Building Inspection Checklist

Masonry & Plaster

Inspection Interval (years)	Chimney (masonry) 1	Brick Walls 2	Stone Walls 2	Stucco Walls 2	Plaster (interior) 2
Cracking:					
—horizontal/vertical	●			●	
—at corners or near windows/doors, roof line		●	●		
—diagonal steps		●	●		
—concrete at foundation		●			
—lintels		●			
—plaster facing (diagonal)		●	●		
—between outside wall and intersection interior wall		●			
—at or between floor levels (horizontal)			●		
Spalling	●	●	●	●	●
Leaking	●	●	●		
Staining:				●	●
—black	●				
—whitish deposits overall or at weepholes		●			
—white or rust color			●		
Leaning or bowing:	●				
—vertically or horizontally outward		●			
—bulging		●	●	●	
—separation from supporting structure		●	●	●	
—settlement			●		
Mortar — erosion from joints	●	●	●		
Local distress over wall openings		●			
Erosion				●	●
Efflorescence		●			
Check-type or large cracks					●
Soft spots					●
Blisters					●
Loosening and falling					●

Table 2.8.2 (continued)

Roofs, Gutters & Downspouts, Flashing, Drains & Sewers, Skylights, Scuttles, Dormers, Flues, Vents

	Slate Roof	Tile Roof	Metal Roof	Bituminous Roof	Gutters/ Downspouts	Flashing	Drains/ Sewers	Skylights, Scuttles, Dormers, Flues and Vents
Inspection Interval (years)	1	1	1	1	1	1	1	1
All roof planes (level and plumb)	●	●	●	●				
Broken, loose, missing or cracked shingles (slate, tile)	●	●						
Corroding, broken, loose fasteners	●	●	●		●	●	●	●
Valley & ridge cap condition	●	●	●	●				
Felt	●	●	●	●				
Deteriorated nailing surface/decking	●		●	●				
Flashing condition	●	●	●	●	●			
Non-adhering or non-elastic cement	●							
Deteriorated battens		●	●					
Buckling			●	●		●		
Roofing paper	●	●	●					
Pitch (only 4 in 12 or more is acceptable)				●				
Cracked soldering (joints & seams)			●		●			●
Gravel				●				
Worn/abraded surface				●				
Bubbling/Cracking/Drying out				●				
Blockage, clogging, corrosion, leaks					●		●	
Insufficient, loose expansion joints					●		●	
Below-grade cleanouts					●			
Strainer condition					●			
Fit of movable parts							●	
Sealants: Disintegration, sagging; bond breakage at side of joints; tearing; bleeding; bulding; excessive softness.						●	●	●
Cracks at bends in sheet metal						●		
Crumbling, powdering of metal						●		
Encrusted metal surfaces						●		
Pitting and corrosion						●		
Blister-like mounds, with inverted "V" cracks in running copper work						●		

Table 2.8.2 (continued)

Interior Structural/Floor Systems

Inspection Interval (years)	Steel Beams, Deck w/Concrete Fill	Reinforced Concrete	Masonry Floors	Wood Joist Floors	Wood Finish Floors	Steel or Cast Iron Columns	Wood Columns
	2	2	2	2	2	2	2
Deflection at midspan; sloping floor	●	●		●			
Connections: corroded, missing	●		●			●	
Bearing at masonry	●			●			
Settlement effects	●			●		●	
Corrosion, mechanical or exterior leakage	●					●	
Spalling: exposed reinforcing steel (floor and celing)		●					
Wide, regularly spaced cracks in floor		●					
Cracks, near and parallel to masonry wall		●					
Surface dusting		●					
Cracked concrete near columns/walls		●					
Leaks			●				
Alterations: new holes cut for stairs, mechanical, etc.			●				
Sidewalk vaults and sub-grade storage			●				
Efflorescence			●				
Cracking at the crown of the arch; between supporting wall and arch			●				
Excessive springiness or vibration				●			
Localized irregularities				●			
Bulging or sagging plaster ceilings				●			
Insect infestation/decay				●			●
Squeaking, worn surface, buckling					●		
Cracking or separation of applied finishes							●
Cracking or bulging masonry infill walls		●					
Noticeable deflection when loaded				●			●
Bowing — out of plumb						●	●
Shrinkage							●
Overloading				●		●	
Lack of restraint on the top in both directions/separation from beams						●	
Loose or missing fireproofing						●	

Table 2.8.2 (continued)

Windows, Doors, Wall Projections and Penetrations (Exterior)

Inspection Interval (years)	Windows & Doors 2	Porticoes 2	Porches 2	Balconies 2	Bay Windows 2	Stoops 2	Cornices 2	Decorative Trim 2
Surface condition of materials	●	●	●	●	●	●	●	●
Condition of coatings and sealants	●	●	●	●	●	●	●	●
Condition of seams and joints, glazing, caulking	●	●	●	●	●	●	●	●
Evidence of horizontal or vertical movement, misalignment		●	●	●	●	●	●	●
Condition of anchorage systems		●	●	●	●	●	●	●
Operation of movable parts and frames	●							
Disease							●	●
Fungus							●	●
Insect infestation/damage							●	●
Rot — dry, wet							●	●

Water is the principal agent of masonry deterioration. Moisture is a catalyst in the mechanical and chemical decay processes of frost and erosion, as well as an inducement to organic deterioration, insect infestation, rot and fungal growth. Moisture travels within masonry in two ways: capillarity, which sucks it to drier areas; and gravity. Recognition of the following forms of deterioration and methods to prevent them from continuing are essential to the preservation of masonry buildings.

ORGANIC CAUSES

Ivy and Creepers

The roots of common ivy (except for the type called "Boston Ivy," which does not disturb the surface) can penetrate the tiniest wall cracks in search of water. As they grow, they can literally break a wall apart. There are some advantages: the roots do dry a wall out and the leaves can shed rain from the building while insulating it in the summertime. However, they also prevent a wall from drying out by shading it from direct sunlight. Highly porous masonry walls should be kept free of vegetation to encourage evaporation.

Creepers do not harm masonry walls and they are, unlike ivy, easy to remove. Creepers should be kept trimmed: runners should not be allowed near windows, soffits, or details. If the creepers cannot be properly maintained, they should be removed.

To properly remove ivy from a masonry structure, the plant should be severed at its roots, and the root system and the ivy on the wall 5 feet up from the ground should be removed. The rest should be allowed to wither, dry, and shrink. The entire plant can then be readily removed. If much resistance is encountered and cutting is necessary, a saw instead of an ax should be used. Disturb the wall no more than is necessary.

Lichens and Mosses

Moist walls are vulnerable to visible, organic growths such as algae, lichens, and mosses and to other microscopic growths which form acids that can affect the surface of masonry. They also retain moisture, causing potential moisture damage to interior plaster or wooden timber or framing elements. Algae can create stains, lichens can obscure details, and mosses, if left unchecked, can block leaders and gutters, causing the water to penetrate the walls. These growths should be removed if damage is evident. Lichens and algae may not be significantly harmful but should be closely and frequently examined.

Bird Droppings

Bird droppings are often found in heavy concentrations on ledges and other typical roosting areas of urban buildings. The low levels of phosphoric and nitric acids can severely damage stone, especially when moistened by rain over long periods of time. In addition, they are visually unpleasant. Removal on a periodic basis is recommended.

MECHANICAL CAUSES

Natural Defects

All stones have natural defects. Sedimentary rock, such as limestone or sandstone, has defects that may result in different degrees of hardness; an uneven surface or splitting of the layers may occur. Minute fissures and cracks in stone can allow penetration of water and salts, inducing decay. Natural stones may also contain other materials which, having different expansion coefficients under thermal stresses, can create cracks and induce failure, especially if surface and the interior temperatures differ greatly.

The presence of soft beds in sedimentary stone results in a more rapid rate of corrosion and a splitting of layers. The alternation of hard and soft layers will produce a characteristic surface roughness even if the stone is properly laid (i.e., made to fit the masonry construction in a position similar to its original riverbed configuration). It is critical when using such stones that the material be utilized in such a manner that the natural bedding plane is perpendicular to the wall's surface. In some cases, entire bedding sheets have spalled. Remedies for this flaw involve complex consolidation techniques or reconstruction.

Improper Stone Combinations

Sandstones adjoining limestones are subjected to deposits of salts from within the stones due to the migration of moisture. If two different limestones abut and one contains the soluble salt magnesium sulfate, efflorescence and exfoliation may result. Frequently, two stones that matched visually when they were installed in a building have since weathered differently and now appear distinctly different. This problem is a critical consideration when replacing existing, deteriorated sandstone with new material of differing characteristics.

Moisture

Masonry materials, especially those of high porosity or low density, such as sandstones or under-fired brick, are exceptionally vulnerable to decay due to moisture. (Refer to Table 3.1.2 for more detail on brick characteristics.) Faulty design or construction may also induce deterioration.

When water freezes, its expansion creates mechanical stresses within the material that can destroy the pores near the surface where wetting is highest. Another disintegration process is caused by seasonal wetting and drying. As water evaporates, any salt elements in solution crystallize, and when the wall is again moistened, new salts are often introduced. Either of these causes may force the more porous masonry materials or stones to spall or to effloresce. Salts can also crystallize behind the surface of the material (especially if the surface is denser than the body of the material or if high winds do not permit evaporation on the surface). This effect is called crypto-efflorescence. Once the excess moisture has been prevented from entering the building, the efflorescence can be brushed off.

Walls should be continually observed for high levels of moisture content, perhaps using special evaluation devices (e.g., moisture meter, chemical filtration paper, and infra-red analysis). The following evaluation sequence should be useful in determining the cause of efflorescence:

1. For older buildings, sudden efflorescence may be a result of repointing within the previous year. Otherwise, construction details should be inspected for new leaks.

2. Location of efflorescence may provide clues to cause. Recent changes in the use of a building or the installation of air conditioning, both likely to effect the presence of moisture in the building, should be considered.

3. The profile and condition of mortar joints, caulking, sealants, flashing, drips, or erosion of mortar at copings and sills should indicate moisture entry points.

4. Wall section and details should indicate path of moisture travel and source of salts. The juncture of wall and roof should be closely inspected.

5. The products of persistent or massive efflorescence should be tested. Identification of salts can be accomplished by X-ray defraction, photographic analysis or chemical analysis.

6. Pipes and drains should be checked for leaks.

7. If inner wall condensation is suspected, testing wall sections may be required.

Wind

Prevailing winds can accelerate the normal wet-dry deterioration cycle. At high wind velocities, a liquid film can be maintained on the masonry surface while evaporation actually takes place within masonry pores, hastening deterioration due to crypto-efflorescence.

In drier or more desert-like areas, however, the erosion caused by the constant bombardment of wind-borne sand can be of significant concern.

Anchor Corrosion

Stone or brick veneers may often be anchored to the bearing wall with metal ties or reinforcing, probably iron, a material which may have been treated with an ineffective protective coating. When the iron anchors rust, their dimensions increase, usually causing the masonry to crack or spall; staining results as well. Proper correction of this failure is a sophisticated and major construction undertaking: the eventual replacement of iron anchors with non-corrosive anchors.

Hard Mortar with Soft Brick

The use of hard mortar with soft brick can result in rapid disintegration of the brick. Since the harder, denser mortar is less permeable than the softer bricks, moisture is trapped within the bricks, making them extremely susceptible to erosion, freeze-thaw cycles, and spalling. Furthermore, the different compressive strengths of the materials make it impossible for the masonry to distribute the stresses evenly across the entire bearing surface. These problems are exaggerated when hard mortar is used to re-point a wall which is predominately of soft mortar. Intense stress near the surface frequently causes crumbling at the arrises or other serious deterioration.

CHEMICAL CAUSES

Pollution is the principal cause of chemically-caused masonry deterioration. Because pollutants are highly soluble in water, they form acids during rain, snow and even high-humidity conditions. Deterioration ensues, especially in areas of a masonry structure which stay wet (e.g., ledges, sculpted detail, etc.), or which are subject to extensive runoff. Atmospheric pollutants include:

Sulphur Compounds

Sulphur compounds are released in the air as soot and smoke from burning fossil fuels. On limestones, sulphur compounds react with the natural carbonate to form a thin impermeable skin of calcium sulphate. This results in blistering, scaling, and spalling. In more serious cases, the sulphur can eat into the crevices of the stone. The harder sandstones and granite show less damage, but they do often build up a thin, harmless hard black film which may be visually undesirable and very difficult to remove.

Sulphur Dioxide

Sulphur dioxide and water combine to form sulphurous acid (H_2SO_3) which chemically reacts with masonry. Smog conditions can actually create sulphuric acid (H_2SO_4) which is aggressively corrosive. Calcium sulphate, a highly soluble salt, is formed by the reaction of sulphur acids and the calcite of mortar, a process which damages stone by hydration processes.

Carbon Dioxide

With water, carbon dioxide forms calcium bicarbonate, a highly soluble salt that causes exfoliation and spalling of masonry through a slow, constant recrystallation process.

Other Pollutants

Other soluble salts that can damage masonry are sodium chloride, sodium sulphate, and sodium hydroxide. These pollutants appear as a powder on the surface of the contaminated stones and foster hydration processes which can result in widespread crumbling. Magnesium sulphate also can create deep cavities in some types of limestone (e.g., dolomite).

All masonry walls contain some moisture because an essential function of most walls is the transmission of vapor, which requires that they not be sealed but be permitted to "breathe." Maintenance of a desirable moisture level therefore involves attempts at control, not outright elimination. The key to alleviating excess moisture is to cut its supply, reduce its flow, and inhibit its movement.

SURFACE TREATMENTS

The most common surface treatment currently in use is the or spray application of a clear liquid silicone "sealer" which generally does not alter the color or texture of the masonry or stone so treated, although it often is discernible as a matte-finish sheen. Paraffin wax, stearic acid, synthetic resin acrylics, and polyvinyl acetate are also acceptable.

The application of silicones accelerates runoff from masonry surfaces, leaving less water to be absorbed, without sealing surface pores, or preventing water from evaporating from the wall face. Silicones may be either water-based or solvent based. Water-based are cheaper, but solvent-based penetrate deeper into the surface. Usually silicones will cause no color change, but if colored mortar is used, test patches left for several weeks can indicate whether bleaching will occur. Depending on the porosity of the surface material and the viscosity of the solution, silicones will penetrate brick 1/8 to 1/4 of an inch.

Note: Silicone surface treatments are only temporarily effective. Localized failures ("spotting") will occur five to seven years after application, arising first in the high runoff areas. Because they eventually "wear off," such silicone solutions are the least damaging surface treatment method currently available.

It is most important to note that although silicones reduce moisture absorptionof the wall surface and permit evaporation of wall moisture through the surface, they do not permit the salts contained in the moisture to pass freely. As the moisture evaporates a crust consisting of these salts may form beneath the masonry surface at the silicone penetration line. Pressures resulting from this subflorescence phenomenon may eventually cause spalling. Extensive testing and analysis is required to fully predict these effects.

The benefits of surface treatments with complex chemical solutions, and all possible risks, have not been fully determined. The long-term effects of changing one of the basic behavioral aspects of a fundamental building material could be very serious. For example: ultraviolet discoloration could occur; or, changing the porosity may tend to trap moisture within the material, increasing the risk of deterioration from repeated freeze-thaw cycles. On the other hand, perhaps it will stabilize moisture conditions and thus retard efflorescence and other salt crystallization.

Because of these uncertainties only surface treatments with water soluble solutions (e.g., silicones and siliconates) should currently be considered for historic buildings. Do not undertake such treatments with acrylic or polymeric solutions (e.g., acrilates), polyvinyl choloride (PVC) or polyvinylacetate (PVA).

MEMBRANE INSTALLATION

Installation of impermeable membranes (e.g., slate, lead, or copper sheet, bitumastic-treated felt, polyethelene) in the mortar joints of masonry walls above grade is a traditional way of stopping moisture migration. Contemporary variations involve drilling closely spaced holes in the wall and inserting liquid epoxy or thermoplastic solutions which harden to form a barrier against moisture movement.

Because of its cost and potentially adverse visual, technical and structural effects, membrane installation is not a recommended practice for GSA personnel to undertake on significant buildings unless expert consultation and technical testing have so indicated.

VENTILATION

Various ventilation techniques have been developed in an attempt to retard or reverse the upward capillary migration of water in masonry. Insertion of devices such as porous "air bricks," syphons and weepholes is generally costly and ineffective; moreover, improper installation of these devices can increase —rather than retard—the flow of water. Their use is not recommended.

ELECTRONIC DRYING

Principles of galvanic action can be applied to masonry walls (i.e., the earth as a conductor and the wall as a battery because the water in the walls is slightly saline in character). Applications of an electric charge reduce the presence of water by de-ionizing the capillaries and reducing their contribution to water migration. Adverse side effects of the process include increased efflorescence and minor shrinkage cracking.

This method is still experimental, and is therefore not recommended.

VENTILATED CAVITIES

If it can be positively determined that excess moisture content is causing harm to the wall structure and its components, a separate interior wall can be erected to provide a continuous ventilated air space. If isolated from the exterior wall and lined with an impervious vapor barrier, this can possibly increase the comfort level for building inhabitants. Such a technique was often executed in traditional materials during construction in the nineteenth century.

Of course, this procedure is only possible if the building interiors are of little value and the entire structure is undergoing a thorough interior renovation.

Caution: Most masonry buildings, especially historic ones, have survived well without elaborate moisture control methods, particularly those involving surface coatings or extensive chemical and electronic treatments. Hasty application of such methods may well have the reverse effect to that intended; for example, a new exterior waterproofing layer may increase interior condensation problems by inhibiting the natural movement of moisture vapor through a wall. Careful analysis is essential to determine the cause, not the symptom, of moisture-related problems. Moreover, test patches for evaluation of coatings do not fully represent the response of a system to such treatments. Accordingly, patient study of analogous treatments on other historic buildings is essential.

The basic advice regarding the treatment of moisture control problems in masonry remains: understand the problem; evaluate the solution; proceed with caution; execute the work carefully; monitor the result; and consult your Regional Historic Preservation Officer.

Movement of building materials is inevitable; if not anticipated in design, cracking will result, particularly in masonry walls which are rigid and inflexible. Before repairs are attempted, three specific items of information must be known: 1) the cause of the cracking; 2) its effect on the performance of the building; and 3) whether movement is complete, incomplete, or intermittent.

CRACKING

The principal causes of masonry cracking and their solutions are:

Temperature Changes

The expansion co-efficient of masonry is relatively low in comparison with those of other common building materials. Consequently, its thermal behavior is unlikely to be a major factor in cracking unless extremely large, unbroken surface areas are involved, or unless masonry is used in areas subject to extreme temperature change (e.g., copings).

Cracking in masonry walls because of temperature changes can be avoided by the use of expansion joints. However, if cracking has occurred, a flexible joint filler should be used; do not re-point, since the joint will have to accommodate future movements.

Ice Formation

The primary danger from ice formation is the phenomenon of "frost heave," the buildup of ice layers in the soil causing it to expand. If foundations are above the frost line, masonry walls will be affected by this expansion, and cracking will result. The only remedial action recommended is to relocate the foundation to a level below the frost line. The likelihood of this type of cracking being discovered in an older building is slight.

Structural Overloading

Cracking that results from structural overloading must be reviewed and diagnosed by a qualified structural engineer, and repairs or remedial action will vary with the engineer's diagnosis.

Ground Overloading Movement

Only a complete analysis by a structural engineer can determine if subsoil settlement or movement is stable or ongoing; a determination will dictate the type of remedial action taken.

Corrosion

Corrosion of ferrous metal elements in a masonry wall (frequently leading to cracking) is caused by moisture, and remedial action should be concerned with discovering the source of that moisture and sealing it. After the corrosion is halted, the cracked masonry can be repaired, generally by repointing, or if the metal is to be replaced, by rebuilding a portion of the wall.

Sulphate Attack

This phenomenon occurs when a gypsum plaster or Keene's cement is used to replace lime in a cement/lime/sand mortar. When moist, the sulphates will expand, causing the masonry to crack.

Remedial action is to remove the faulty mortar and to replace it with a proper cement/lime/sand mixture.

CRITERIA FOR MASONRY PRESERVATIVES

Masonry preservatives should be used cautiously. Absolute prohibition of such processes is not warranted; they are frequently a useful part of a preservation maintenance program. However, **the application of any treatment to the masonry surface of a building involves potential risks which should be the subject of careful research and testing, frequently including laboratory analysis and consultant advice.**

The following criteria are useful in the selection of masonry preservative treatments:

Depth of Penetration

Effective preservatives must reach beneath the masonry surface to achieve a secure bond, not just to form a hard exterior crust; in general, deeper penetration is required for low-density, high-porosity masonry materials.

Permeability

Preservatives are usually intended to shed water (i.e., to prevent penetration from the exterior); however, they must do so in a "one way" manner, without filling all pores, so that moisture will not be entrapped in the masonry.

Coefficient of Expansion

To prevent surface deterioration from differential expansion and contraction, a preservative must possess either a similar rate of movement as the masonry to which it is applied, or it must remain sufficiently elastic to accept such movement.

Corrosibility and Toxicity

A preservative must be harmless to the treated masonry, to adjacent surfaces and to plants, animals and humans who may come in contact either with the material or runoff from the masonry surface.

Solubility

To remain effective over a long period of exterior exposure, a masonry preservative should not be readily soluble in water, or subject to moisture deterioration.

Appearance

Masonry surface treatments, even those heralded as "colorless," frequently alter the natural appearance of the material itself or the joints (e.g., texture, reflectance, color, etc.); test patches are essential to determine impact on appearance.

Longevity

Even the most durable treatments currently require reapplication every 5-7 years.

Ease of Application

The most frequent application methods utilize brushes or spray equipment; occasionally, heating of the preservative or other special steps are necessary (e.g., prior cleaning, surface repairs, vacuum application, etc.); check for the degree of worker's skill required and the necessity for staging, protection of adjacent surfaces, etc.

Economy

The first coat of preservative treatments should be reviewed in comparison to their longevity and the severity of the problem prompting their use.

TYPES OF PRESERVATIVES

Despite a wide variety of trade names and manufacturers, masonry preservatives fall into the following types:

Paint

If not built-up, a good oil or lime paint will permit the wall to breathe and moisture to evaporate. However, numerous paint layers or use of nonporous paints (e.g., epoxies) can lead to problems of entrapped moisture, including peeling, spalling, and crypto-efflorescence.

Oils

Oils (such as linseed oils) will dry to a tough coating and will seal the pores of the masonry material. However, even if no pigment is added to the oil, it will, in time, darken the material. Since this does seal masonry pores, crypto-efflorescence and spalling may result.

Waxes

Waxes must be applied to the masonry in a solvent vehicle or molten state. Best penetration results if the masonry can be heated, but not to the point that vaporization of entrapped or hydroscopic moisture could occur, causing fractures or spalling. Waxes may also melt and flow from the stone in hot summer weather. Small removable masonry objects, such as statuary, may be immersed in a bath of molten wax under carefully controlled conditions, but because the wax seals masonry pores it is not recommended for exterior use.

Silicones

Silicones and siliconates: Refer to Section 3.1.2, Moisture Control in Masonry.

Calcium Carbonate

Calcium carbonate, an alkaline imparted to stone by calcium hydroxide (lime wash), is susceptible to attack by atmospheric sulphur. Acids which recombine with the calcium carbonate form salts of sulphur. The calcium sulfite or calcium sulfate that is formed is soluble, and deterioration proceeds as with the original stone.

Alkaline Earth Hydroxides

Both strontium hydroxide and barium hydroxide can be used instead of calcium hydroxide. These alkaline earth hydroxides, which react with atmospheric carbon dioxide, deposit carbonates in the stone that also react with atmospheric sulphur acids. However, these particular strontium and barium sulfites and sulfates are insoluble in water and therefore halt deterioration. Unfortunately, as with limewash, the surface reacts first, thereby limiting further penetration to appropriate depths.

STONE OR MASONRY CONSOLIDATION

The preservation and conservation of deterioration stone or masonry may require consolidation of the material to: 1) preserve the exterior surfaces and detail; 2) increase its resistance to water penetration; and 3) diminish its susceptibility to attack by aggressive agents (e.g., carbon dioxide, sulphur dioxide, nitrous dioxide, etc.).

Caution: Stone consolidation is a highly specialized procedure. If stone or masonry consolidation appears warranted, special consultants should be retained to assist in the analysis, design, and implementation. In most cases, replacement of damaged stone with new stone will prove to be a less costly and an equally acceptable alternative.

The exterior cleaning of buildings has frequently led to serious, sometimes irreversible, surface damage. This Guide discusses the underlying issues, available techniques, and proper procedures for exterior cleaning. It cannot provide complete or final guidance on such a complex subject. The watchwords for an exterior cleaning decision are care and caution. Consult your Regional Historic Preservation Officer.

GENERAL CLEANING PRINCIPLES

Before undertaking any masonry cleaning, consider these questions:

Why clean?

Exterior masonry cleaning should be motivated by sound technical reasons: to remove harmful surface deposits, to retard future deterioration, to accurately restore an appearance. Before you focus on **how** to clean, know **why**.

What is to be removed?

"Dirt" could be soil, soot, smoke, organic matter, animal feces, metal stains, solids from air pollution, oil elements from within the masonry itself, or a variety of other chemical and organic products. More probably, it is a complex combination of several types of foreign matter each of which may require a discrete cleaning method. Analysis of this issue is an essential step in forming a proper cleaning program.

What is the surface?

The interaction between the masonry material itself and the foreign matter which contaminates it are also essential items for study. The surface which will remain after cleaning must be the top preservation priority. Analysis of the surface should include potential adverse effects of various cleaning techniques, the most efficient means for breaking the bond between the dirt and surface, the results of previous cleaning attempts, waterproofing or similar repairs.

What will it cost?

Beyond establishing the mere cost of the cleaning operations, the answer to this question will relate the expense involved to the potential risk incurred, and maintenance.

What is the risk?

Any exterior masonry cleaning operation involves some risk; it may not work properly, or it may damage the surface.

Is it worth it?

Risk, cost, and benefit must be related in any maintenance or repair decision. In preservation maintenance, the balance must weigh in favor of "doing no harm." Administration of historic resources involves the occasional recognition that deciding not to act can be a constructive course.

EVALUATING CLEANING
PROCEDURES

In selecting an appropriate masonry cleaning technique, adhere to the following general procedure: 1) Determine type and nature of soiling (includes sampling, laboratory testing for chemical composition, comparative analysis of elements present, etc.); 2) Determine type and character of stone or brick (includes archival research, historical study, technical testing for abrasion resistance, hardness, staining properties, etc.); 3) Consider local site conditions (includes analysis of environment surrounding the building, rain runoff patterns and composition, etc.); 4) Consider cost and schedule of operation; 5) Determine degree of cleanliness desired (if removing the crusty coat removes the original exterior finish, the result will be an appearance that will never be close to the original)? 6) Conduct test patches to determine probable effects, remembering that short-term tests to determine long-term effects are risky. 7) Assess compliance of materials and procedures with relevant codes and standards (e.g., with OSHA).

TECHNIQUES

There are three basic methods of cleaning exterior masonry: 1) water cleaning, 2) abrasive cleaning, and 3) chemical cleaning. A fourth, involving highly sophisticated electronic technology, is emerging, but it is not yet in widespread use. Within each category, a variety of techniques is common, and frequently combinations of procedures and methods are used on one project. (Table 3.1.1 briefly compares various exterior cleaning techniques.)

REMOVAL OF STAINS

Certain persistent stains will not be removed from a masonry or stone surface in the course of an otherwise successful exterior cleaning operation. If complete removal is warranted (in some instances, it may be best to leave the stain), use the following specific recommendations: 1) **Always** conduct a test in an unobtrusive location, allowing post-test evaluation time before tackling the entire job; 2) Never use a solution which is stronger, or a technique which is harsher, than the minimum required to do the job; 3) Protect adjacent surfaces, shrubs, passersby, etc.; 4) Be very skeptical about commercial cure-alls and proprietary processes.

PAINT REMOVAL FROM MASONRY

Before attempting to remove paint from a masonry surface, evaluate the answers to these basic questions influencing the removal effort:

Why was it painted in the first place?

Paint has often been used to waterproof or to consolidate low-quality or deteriorating masonry. Many surfaces may have been intentionally painted; in these cases, the workmanship and jointing, if revealed, may be poor quality and unsightly.

What type of paint is it? What is its condition?	Make every reasonable attempt to determine the type of paint, its age, its condition, and the number of layers; this will take much of the guesswork out of the removal effort. Where extensive removal is contemplated, professional examination of scrapings may be warranted; often, this service can be obtained from a reputable manufacturer's laboratory, by mail, at no cost.
What is the condition of the masonry surface beneath the paint?	Inspection of a painted surface can sometimes reveal important clues to the subsurface condition, which will be affected by some removal processes. Is the mortar sound or powdery (probe it to check)? Is the masonry surface spalling? Is there discoloration or blistering of the paint which would indicate trapped moisture or rusting anchors? Are fresh cracks (i.e., non-painted) evident? Other indicators of surface condition may be found by searching for unpainted portions (e.g., behind shutters, trim, sheet metal assemblies, etc.), or by inspecting the rear surface of the wall.
Why remove the paint at all?	Often, paint removal is undertaken to create a "natural" or "original" look which is erroneous; satisfy yourself that this situation does not exist before proceeding with removal operations. Frequently, proper surface preparation and repainting can be accomplished promptly, at less cost, and with far less damage to the structure than paint removal.
TEST APPLICATIONS	Test applications of propsed removal techniques and materials should be made before proceeding with the entire job. Select small, unobtrusive locations for the tests which are representative of the range of conditions to be confronted; take photographs and samples; monitor the procedures closely so that they may be repeated accurately; vary the removal process based upon a careful evaluation of results.
PAINT REMOVAL TECHNIQUES	Mechanical methods, similar to those discussed in Table 3.1.1, are often successfully used to remove paint from masonry (subject to the usual reservations about the ill effects of these methods when improperly applied):
Abrasion	Common methods include stiff bristle brushes, wire brushes, or steel wool.
Dry/Wet Blasting	Grits used, in addition to silica, include ground walnut shells and small glass beads, called "micro bubbles." **Blasting in any form is discouraged, and should only be undertaken upon competent professional advice.**
Heat	Using a torch or electric heating element. **Note:** This technique will frequently damage all but the most durable masonry ma-

terials by heating the entrapped moisture vapor near the surface so rapidly that expansion will cause fractures of the stone material; however, with a stone of uniform density, such as granite, this method may be acceptable.

Solvent Removers

The most common paint removal method is the application of a solvent, by brush or spray, followed by a water rinse or application of another neutralizing chemical. Application techniques vary too widely to permit a standard specification; manufacturer's recommendations and test observations must be used. In applying any remover, take extreme care to protect adjacent architectural elements (e.g., windows, metalwork, etc.), natural features (e.g., shrubs, trees, etc.), as well as workmen and passers-by.

SELECTION OF PAINT REMOVERS

The following general guidelines will assist in the selection of proper paint removers for most cases:

Calcimine Paint

Remove with water, under moderate pressure, with mechanical abrasion as required.

Oil-based paint (including boiled linseed technique)

Remove with commercially-available alkaline removers (not 100% lye). Note: rinse repeatedly with water; avoid application of waterproofing agents for at least several months after removal.

Latex-based Paint

Remove with commercially-available mineral spirit solvents.

Epoxy

Remove per manufacturer's recommendations. This type is highly resistant to removal, bonds extremely well to masonry, and will be troublesome.

Cement (e.g., "waterglass" binder of potassium and calcium silicates)

Abrasion removal (augmented with solvents as for latex paints above) is suggested.

REMOVAL OF MASONRY STAINS

Copper/Bronze

Stains are most often found in areas affected by runoff from copper flashing, gutters or fasteners; occasionally found adjacent to bronze statuary or architectural bronze (e.g., doors, frames, hardware, etc.).

Mix dry one part ammonium chloride (or sal ammonia water) and four parts powdered talc. Add ammonia water and stir until a thick paste is obtained. Using only wooden or non-metallic tools, apply to stain and let dry. Remove when dry and reapply until stain is removed. Flush well with water upon completion.

Iron

Caused by rusting cast iron or steel either adjacent to or embedded in the masonry.

Brush a solution of oxalic acid in water (one pound per gallon). Ammonium bifluoride (½ pound per gallon) will hasten the reaction; however, proceed with caution, as the ammonium bifluoride generates hydrofluoric acid which may etch the brick. It should be used with much caution and should be tested in a small patch before using.

Alternatively, a solution of seven parts lime-free glycerine, one part sodium citrate, and six parts warm water with whiting or Kisel for thickening can be applied to the surface and removed when dry. Repeat until the stain has disappeared. Rinse thoroughly afterward with water. Brown stains that do not respond are probably manganese stains.

Lichens and Mosses

Caused by organic action on damp masonry, generally in shady or intermittently sunlit locations.

Lichens and mosses can be killed with a solution of zinc or magnesium silica fluoride (one part to 40 parts water) or a commercial weed killer. Green stains that do not respond are probably vanadium stains. The presence of lichens and mosses indicates damp walls which should be continually observed.

Manganese

Caused by impurities in brick manufacture. Manganese stains usually appear on mortar joints. They have a brown, oily appearance and seem to run down the interface of the masonry unit and the mortar. Such stains are common especially when manganese grey or brown brick have been used.

Remove with a solution of one part by volume of acetic acid (80 per cent or stronger), one part hydrogen peroxide (30 to 34 per cent), six parts water. The stain may recur as quickly as within a few days, but harsher chemicals will do excessive damage to mortar and masonry materials and therefore are not recommended.

Oil and Tar

Found on areas beneath or adjacent to tar and gravel roofs; also occur at grade from asphalt roadway splatter.

Commercially available emulsifying agents can often be used to remove oil and tar stains. Kerosene can also be mixed with the oil and tar and then rinsed with water or steam. A poultice of benzene, naphtha, or trichloroethylene can also effectively remove oil stains. Carbon tetrachloride is also effective.

Paint

Caused by painters' drops and spills; graffiti (especially spray cans).

As a general remedy, apply a solution of trisodium phosphate (one part to 5 parts water by weight). Let the paint soften and remove it. Wash with soapy water and rinse thoroughly with clean water. Some commerical paint removers can be safely used but they should be tested before application. (See preceding detailed discussion of paint removal in this Section.)

Vanadium

Stain is usually green although it can also appear brownish-green or even brown. The source of vanadium stains in masonry units is not altogether certain; impurities within the masonry itself or interaction with vanadium alloys in fasteners and anchors is suspected. They frequently become apparent only when the masonry is cleaned chemically. For this reason when cleaning masonry chemically, test patches should be made to determine detrimental side effects.

To remove green stains simply, use sodium hydroxide.

The following neutralization process should be followed: 1) after cleaning, rinse thoroughly with water; 2) apply a solution of ½ pound of potassium or sodium hydroxide to one quart of water with a brush and let set for two to three days; 3) hose off the white hydroxide salt with water.

Caution: Vanadium stains should never be washed with hydrochloric acid, which fixes them and turns them brown. Brown stains can be removed with a caustic soda solution, but the potential damage to masonry is severe.

Wood

Brown or grey wood stains are caused by tannin or resin from the wood spreading across a masonry surface, usually in water run-off.

Scrub the surface, using non-metallic brushes, with a solution of oxalic acid (one part to 40 parts hot water).

Welding Splatter

Caused by adjacent welding operations.

Scrape as much of the metal from the masonry as possible. Apply a poultice of the remedy prescribed for iron stains. Remove when dry and reapply until the stain is removed.

Table 3.1.1
Comparison of Masonry Cleaning Techniques

Category	Technique	Characteristics	Technical Details	Suitable Surfaces	Advantages	Disadvantages
Abrasive	Hand scrubbing	Simplest method. Hard work. Best for details and small areas.	Stiff, non-metallic brushes preferred. Power tools can help, if properly used.	Hard surfaced or polished materials; unit masonry.	Safe. Effective.	Labor-intensive expensive. Requires staging or swing bucket.
Electronic	High intensity lights	Use of laser pulses or Xenon flashes to selectively disintegrate soiling and stains.	Highly experimental.	Masonry; under evaluation.	High degree of control of effects; under evaluation.	Unknown; further testing required.
Water Cleaning	Soaking	Near-pure water flowing across a masonry surface for an extended time period. For soiling only; not suitable for complex stains.	No pressure; lengthy duration. Wetting agents frequently added.	Soft, porous stones (e.g., sandstone, marble, old concrete, etc.).	Safe, quiet. Does not require skilled personnel.	Slow. Ground saturation likely. Seasonal.
Water Cleaning	Pressure cleaning	near-pure water under pressure.	Medium pressures preferred (200-600 psi). Frequently involves use of heated water, chemical additives, etc.	Sound, undeteriorated stone and brick of moderate to firm density; jointing must be equally able to withstand penetrating pressures.	Effective for most soiling and stains. Relatively safe (if pressures are carefully controlled). Inexpensive.	Requires skilled personnel. Can cause secondary damage to interior surfaces, metal anchors wood members, etc. Seasonal.
Water Cleaning	Steam cleaning	Washing with steam under low pressure.	Low pressure (10-30 psi).	Most stone and brick. Especially good for sculpture and detail.	Relatively safe. Effective.	Hazardous to workers. Expensive. Cumbersome equipment. Seasonal. Difficult to control over large surfaces; "splotchy" appearance.

Table 3.1.1 (continued)

Category	Technique	Characteristics	Technical Details	Suitable Surfaces	Advantages	Disadvantages
Water Cleaning	Acid cleaning	Brush or spray applied solution; water rinse.	Strength: 5% max. Common agents are muriatic (hydrochloric), phosphoric & hydrofluoric acids.	Igneous stones (granite) concrete, and glazed brick. Some calcareous sandstones.	Effective especially for complex soiling and stains. Inexpensive. Speedy.	Risk of spotting, bleaching, and efflorescence. Damage is irremediable. Can etch adjacent glass or metal, destroy landscaping, etc. Seasonal.
Water Cleaning	Alkaline cleaning	As above.	Strength as above. Common agents are sodium or potasium hydroxide, and caustic soda.	Carbonate stones (limestone and marble).	As above.	Risk of crystallization & efflorescence. Damage is irremediable. Seasonal.

SOURCES OF BRICK FOR HISTORIC MATCH

Contemporary and Reproduction Brick

Many manufacturers carry a variety of reproduction brick as well as some standard lines that come quite close in visual character to some earlier brickwork. If exact matches are not available, sufficient quantity brick purchases will allow special shapes to be fabricated and adjustments in other characteristics. (Full kiln amounts, usually a minimum of 20,000 bricks, are required to justify the special order at a reasonable price.)

Relocated Brick

It may be possible to use original bricks from other, less visible areas of the building, replacing them with standard brick. Relocated bricks should be identical to those on the replacement wall, and must be exterior brick on the exterior face. In limited cases, sawing these bricks in half can make them go farther. Turn the cut face of the brick to the inside of the wall, exposing only the original faces. This procedure is possible only if the brick is dense enough to survive cutting, and if the brick face opposite the exterior is in good condition and cleanable. Cutting bricks may be especially practical if one side of damaged bricks remains intact, but generally such cutting and replacement is feasible only if the mortar has a lime composition. Removing hard Portland cement mortar would probably damage brick surfaces and arrises.

Salvaged Brick

Bricks from other local buildings of the same period that have been demolished might be useful replacements, but take care to test for technical compatibility and matched appearance.

Synthetic Brick

Field fabrication of a small number of replacement brick may be possible in limited circumstances, preferably for the more homogeneous Victorian brick. This method requires cutting back deteriorated brick to expose sound material. The areas can then be built up again, using a specially designed composite, often a mixture of original brick dust and an appropriate resin. This craft combines the most demanding talents of mason, sculptor, and chemist. It is **costly and experimental**, but may be worth considering for important buildings, in visually critical areas.

Painted Brick

As a last resort, if the visual character of a brick cannot be matched, insert a technically compatible unit and paint the surface to match. This readily attainable technique is demanding, and will require repainting periodically to prevent visual deterioration.

DESIGN CRITERIA FOR MATCHING BRICK

Size and Uniformity

A match is necessary in all dimensions: length, width, and height. The percentage of variation in the size of the brick also is important. If the original wall contains considerable size variation, using uniformly sized brick will result in an apparent mismatch. A section of brickwork should be studied to obtain a representative range of size variation. Reproductions of late eighteenth and early nineteenth century brick are readily available; a match for the high quality and precision of mid- to late-nineteenth century brickwork is not. (See Table 3.1.2.)

In brick sizes, the normal proportion in practice is: one stretcher length equals three brick thicknesses plus two joints or two brick widths plus one joint. (See Figure 3.1.2.) The majority of GSA's significant older buildings utilize standard sizes of brick. Formally adopted in 1899 by the National Brickmaker's Association, they are:

Common brick: 8-1/4 by 4 by 3-1/4 inches
Face brick: 8-3/8 by 4 by 2-3/8 inches

In general, other unit masonry elements in the GSA inventory (e.g., concrete block, cast block, tile, etc.), follow a comparable dimension format, using 8-inch vertical coursing.

Color and Range

No one variable is more important in obtaining a visual match in old and new brickwork than color range. Where this occurs both major and minor colors should be used in amounts and in pattern equal to the original.

Finish

Brick also has a wide range of finish textures, each reflecting light differently. The finish texture of brick is important to the color match.

Arrises or Edges

Arrises range in shape from those in Victorian brickwork, which were crisp, sharp, and even, to those in most eighteenth century brick which were rough, rounded, and uneven. Modern extruded brick, depending upon the quality of manufacture, varies in quality from rough to fairly even.

Technical Compatibility

Where the scale of the project is large enough to justify the expenditure, technical testing should be used to determine the structural compatibility of new and original brick. Old and new brick must react similarly to weathering and wear if the structural integrity of the composite wall is to be maintained. Important characteristics involve: a) absorption of water; b) evaporation of water; c) volumetric changes due to wetting and freezing; and d) compressive strength.

MATCHING STONE

The following criteria should be considered in the matching of stone:

Type of Stone

i.e., granite, limestone, brownstone, and marble.

Overall Color Appearance

Where several hues appear within a stone, the overall color is a blend which the eye creates from all the separate colors (i.e., pink, sandy, grey, cream, etc.).

Individual Colors and Percent of Uniformity

Remember that a replacement stone which is the same type as the original may not be the same color because it will have been quarried in a different location. If the difference is severe, locate another stone which is coincidentally a closer match to the color and pattern of the original stone.

Pattern

Strong patterns normally occur in natural stone, particularly in marbles; more uniform patterns also occur, such as travertine, which is uniformly off-white. Granites range from a strong pattern to a uniform one, but, in general, they are much more uniform than marbles. Limestone and sandstone taken from any single source appear essentially uniform; however, such stones quarried from different areas exhibit wide color variations. The sandstone currently quarried and termed "brownstone," for example, ranges from dark brown to near pink in color. Natural brownstone suitable for matching stone used in many Victorian structures can be obtained from England; it is virtually unavailable from quarries in the United States today.

Shape and Size

New stone must match the original in the general size of the blocks, the variation in block sizes, and the pattern in which it is laid.

Finish

Finishes are an important variable affecting the appearance of stone structures. Machine finishes presently range from polished, through honed, wirecut, and flame-finished to rough cut; properly used, they can match quite closely many of the finishes prevalent in the nineteenth century.

Cleanliness of Original Surface

Stonework should always be matched in as clean a state as possible, and if cleaning the original surface is not planned when undertaking new stonework sufficient areas should be cleaned to allow proper identification and match of stone work.

SLATE

Most slate can be closely, if not identically, matched. In replacing a slate roof, reuse as many of the original slates as possible, placing them in areas that are visible from the street. New slate then can be placed on the least visible areas or on roof slope areas separate from those where original slate is reused. Select new high quality slate low in carbonates and iron sulphide.

Slate can be ordered in matching thicknesses and sizes when rectangular shapes are involved. Suppliers may produce some special shapes; cutting special shapes can be done on the job site.

Table 3.1.2
Comparative Characteristics of Brick Types

Type of Brick	Handmade	Hand Pressed	Victorian Machine Pressed	Modern, Extruded Wire Cut
Period of Manufacture	1750-1850	1825-1875	1875-1910	1900-Present
Color	Red, yellow, orange, buff, brown, grey to blue grey to black	Moderate to dark red	Dark red, brown	Varies
Color range	Broad range	Fairly uniform	Very uniform	Moderate Range
Texture	Sandy	Sandy	Smooth	Varies from smooth to somewhat irregular
Surface Condition	Undulating, occasional projections, pitting	Even and consistent	Even and Smooth	Even to some pitting
Arrises, edges	Soft, uneven	Crisp	Extremely sharp crisp, regular	Crisp to moderately crisp
Size	Wide variation	Little variation	Identical	Little variation (standard tolerance ± 1/8" for 8" stretcher)
Physical composition	High mineral content	Little mineral content	Low mineral content	Varies (with manufacturer and applicable ASTM grade standard)

The following criteria should be considered when matching mortar:

Color

Matching the color of old mortar must be done: either on site or by laboratory analysis. When examined in place, the existing mortar should be cleaned or the face scraped away to reveal the original color, undisturbed by weathering. Laboratory analysis also can determine the proper coloring additives of the new mortar. Such mix formulae are important to later work and should be filed. After the new mortar is applied and set, brush the joint to expose the color which may be obscured by the cementing agent. When lime is a mix ingredient, commercial cement coloring agents must be analyzed, because they may alter the basic mortar mix characteristics. Mortar colors should be particles of stable (preferably inorganic) compounds and should never exceed 15 per cent of the cement by weight. If carbon black is used, it should not exceed 3 per cent of the weight of the cement. (See Tables 3.1.3 and 3.1.4.)

Note: However historically accurate, harmful additives, such as salt (for lowering the freezing point) and sugar (for retarding the set), should not be used.

Composition

Where major repointing of lime-sand mortar is done, the appropriate mortar should be determined by chemical analysis of the original, or chemical and physical analysis of the bricks or stone. For smaller projects, a variation of traditional recipes may be prescribed, although use of a nontested material should be limited to areas where an adverse effect will not compromise the historic character of the structure. A small portion of Portland cement may be added to increase strength and durability, but this ingredient should never exceed one-twelfth of the total lime-sand mixture.

In repointing, a good hydrated lime should be used with a clean and sharp sand. The coarseness, color, and type of new sand should match the original. That match can be determined either by laboratory analysis or by crushing a sample of the original mortar, mixing it with water, and retrieving the sand residue. Take care to identify the **original mortar** rather than the repointing mortar or the overcoat of plaster or stucco.

JOINTS

Any renovation work involving mortar should attempt to duplicate the characteristics of the original mortar and joint unless it can be proven that the original was a poor choice, or unless conditions have altered significantly since original construction. Appearance and performance are more important than duplication of constituent elements, and it is possible to match mortar visually without matching its chemical make-up. Mismatched pointing is visually disruptive.

Good mortar joints should: 1) Bind masonry units; 2) Seal the wall from weathering forces; 3) Compensate for dimensional variation of units; 4) Absorb minor wall movement; and 5) Provide a decorative effect to the wall surface.

All types of mortar joints fall into two basic categories (see Figures 3.1.3 and 3.1.4):

Trowelled Joints

Weathered Joints are the best of the trowelled joints; they are compacted and shed water easily.

Flush Joints are not compacted and even leave a hairline crack when the excess mortar is cut away. The joint is not always watertight.

Struck Joints are compacted somewhat, but are not impermeable. The small ledge left on the brick retains, rather than sheds, water.

Tooled Joints

Concave and V-Shaped Joints are effective in resisting rain penetration, and are especially useful in areas of high winds and heavy rains.

Raked Joints are compacted somewhat, but are not weathertight and probably should not be used where high winds, heavy rains, and freezing occur. Raked joints produce marked shadows and tend to darken the overall appearance of a wall. Raked joints are frequently tuck pointed with a colored or other decorative mortar.

Raised Joints, which are quite rare, are made with a trowel and straight edge.

Ruled Joints are usually combined with another type of tooled joint. A line along the center of the joint makes the joint appear smaller.

Beaded Joints are made with a special tool which molds the mortar to a projecting profile.

Special Joint Treatments

Special jointing treatments may occasionally occur in GSA's historic buildings, especially on the interior; they include:

Stippling is a treatment given any mortar joint, plaster, stucco, or painted surface by touching it with the end of a stiff brush before it completely sets. The purpose is to give new surfaces the worn appearance of older surfaces.

Pencilling provides an appearance of even and continuous joints on brick or stone walls. Joints are merely traced with a white or cream-colored paint in a narrow line. The paint, usually a lime paint, should be compatible with whatever paint is used on the remaining surface.

STONE JOINTS

The irregularity of pattern and thickness in much stone work (especially random rubble) calls for various joint treatments (see Figure 3.1.4): the mortar might be brought flush with the stone; the entire wall might be stuccoed; or the mortar might be scored. Unusual joint profiles were often added, and raised or V-shapes were common. Sometimes joints were galleted, or accented, by pushing pebbles into the mortar. For ashlar work, the mortar joints were usually subordinated to other stone surface features, such as rustication.

JOINT PREPARATION FOR REPOINTING

Effective repointing requires that existing mortar be removed from masonry joints, usually to a minimum depth of 3/4-inch. This operation frequently leads to severe, irreparable damage of the masonry surface unless extreme care is taken.

A variety of techniques have been developed for routing joints:

Recommended Routing Techniques

Brushing. Soft mortars can frequently be removed merely by brushing the joints with a stiff fiber bristle brush; this method is extremely safe.

Blowing/Washing. Compressed air or water under moderate pressures (not exceeding 500 psi), can remove most soft mortars and deteriorated hard mortars. Little surface damage will result if care is taken to control the pressures and suitable pretesting is successfully accomplished.

Hand Chiseling. Use of hand chisels is the least damaging technique for cutting out joints. Specially manufactured chisels should fit the width of the joints. Although this task is difficult, time-consuming, and therefore expensive, it is the least harmful way to remove stubborn hard mortars.

Not Recommended

Power Chiseling or Vibrating. Pneumatic chisels or power tools which use high tension vibrating needles, called descalers, have been used for mortar removal. However, controlling these tools requires great skill, and they can knock edges and corners off delicate brickwork. The repointing will look sloppy, and the mortar joints will be widened, permanently altering the overall appearance of the wall.

Rotary Saws or Disks. Not recommended for historic buildings: the most common, and potentially the most injurious, technique of removing mortar from masonry joints is to cut it out with a machine powered revolving carborundum disk. It is difficult to use this technique without damaging the edges of the masonry, widening the joints significantly, and altering the appearance and performance of the wall.

FIGURE 3.1.1
BRICK BONDS AND JOINTS

BRICK BONDS

BRICK JOINTS

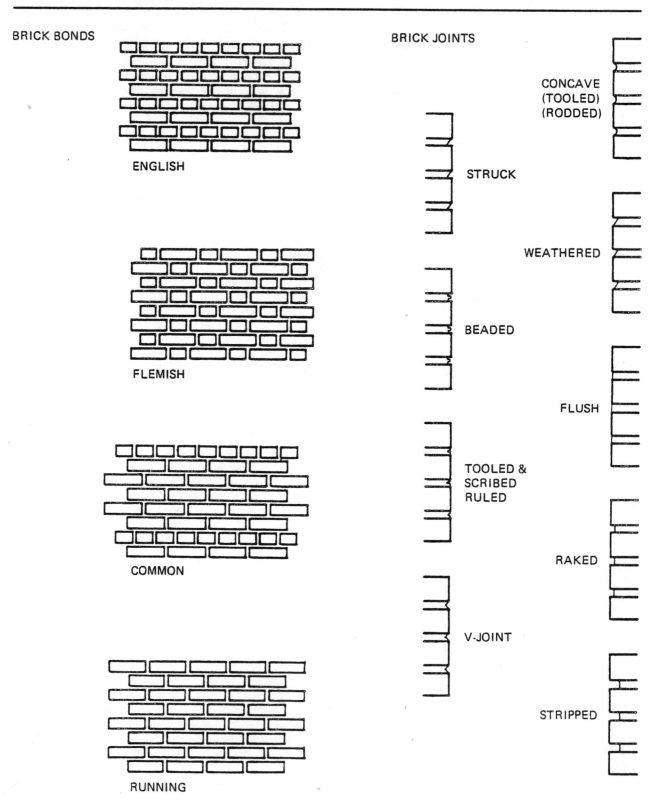

ENGLISH

FLEMISH

COMMON

RUNNING

CONCAVE
(TOOLED)
(RODDED)

STRUCK

WEATHERED

BEADED

FLUSH

TOOLED &
SCRIBED
RULED

RAKED

V-JOINT

STRIPPED

FIGURE 3.1.2
STONE JOINTS

STONE LAYOUTS

STONE JOINTS

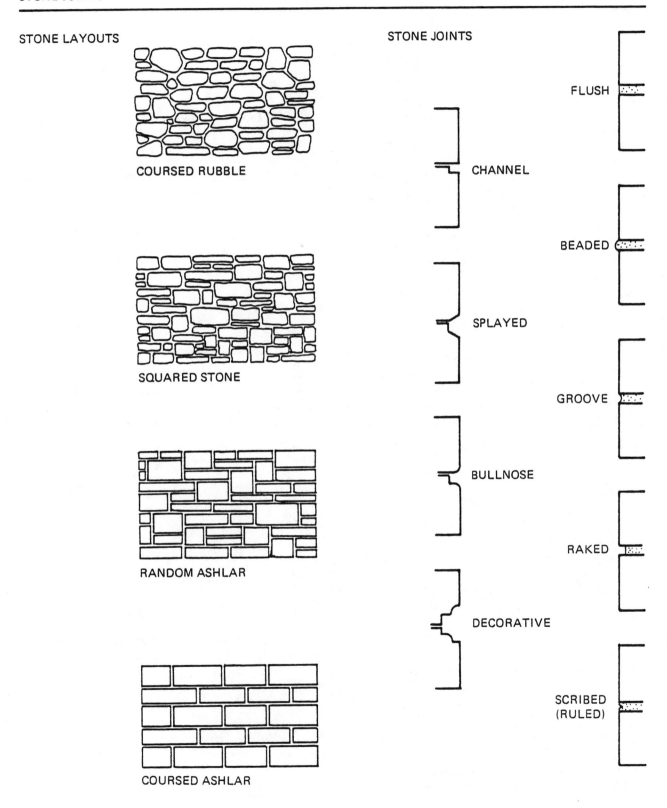

COURSED RUBBLE

SQUARED STONE

RANDOM ASHLAR

COURSED ASHLAR

CHANNEL

SPLAYED

BULLNOSE

DECORATIVE

FLUSH

BEADED

GROOVE

RAKED

SCRIBED
(RULED)

Table 3.1.3
Recommended Cement—Lime Mortars

	Ratio of Cement to Lime	ASTM Type	Use
Clay Brick or Clay Tile Units:	1:1/4	M	Below grade
	1:1/2 — 1 1/4	N	Above
	1:1/4 — 2 1/2	O	General interior use
	1:2	O	External walls, moderate exposure spring and summer construction
	1:1	N	External walls, severe exposure all seasons
	1:2 or 1:3	O K	Internal, spring and summer
	1:2 or 1:2	N O	Internal, autumn and winter
Sand — Lime Brick:	1:1	N	External, severe exposure, all seasons
	1:2 or 1:3	O K	Internal, spring and summer
	1:1 or 1:2	N O	Internal, autumn and winter
	1:1 — 1 1/4	N	Ordinary service
	1:0 — 1/4	M	Heavy loading, severe frost action
	1:1/4	M	
	1:1/4 — 1/2	S	
Porous Limestone or Sandstone:	1:3	K	
Dense Limestone or Sandstone:	1:1	N	

Note: Lime serves also as a "plasticizer"
From: National Research Council, Canada

Table 3.1.4
Mortar Specifications

Property Specifications		Proportion Specifications			Total
Mortar Type	Min. Comp. Strength PSI	Cement	Lime	Sand	
K	75	1	2 ¼ — 4		1:3:12
O	350	1	1 ¼ — 2 ½	2 to 3 times sum of cement and lime volumes	1:2:9
N	750	1	½ — 1 ¼		1:1:6
S	1800	1	¼ — ½		1:½:4 ½
M	2500	1	¼ min.		1:¼:3

From: National Lime Association

TERRA COTTA DETERIORATION

Tentative conclusions about the causes of terra cotta deterioration include: faulty materials; faulty craftmanship; improper detailing; thermal forces; windloading; moisture; efflorescence; anchor corrosion; and chemical forces.

Most damage to terra cotta is done by improper cleaning methods. Never use strong acids (e.g., hydrofluoric) to clean terra cotta.

REPAIR METHODS FOR TERRA COTTA

Besides the patching and standard repointing techniques discussed in Section 3.1.6, a number of special actions can be considered.

Frequently, the proper installation of relieving joints might be necessary to alleviate the high pressures that can occur in the material. Location and design will depend upon the specific circumstances. Material failure is usually not too extensive and most likely to be limited to deterioration of the glaze. Depending upon the extent and type, replacement might be necessary, by removing the existing glaze and applying new coatings with a similar appearance. Partial patching and repair is technically possible but should be limited to low-visibility areas of buildings because of the difficulty of producing a consistent, visually acceptable finish.

Exact replacement of terra cotta is usually quite expensive because reproduced elements cannot be directly cast. In some instances, replacement and repair with other materials is suggested. This would require special design solutions and can range from replacement with large precast concrete panels to sections duplicated in fiberglass. Solutions will depend upon condition, extent, details and configuration of the building and its facade.

Caution: The repair methods discussed here for terra cotta are technically complex and, if improperly executed, could have an irreversible adverse effect. Consult your RHPO when contemplating such actions.

CAST CONCRETE AND CAST STONE

A number of GSA buildings, principally from the early twentieth century, use cast stone or cast concrete for veneer panels, trim, architectural detail (frequently bas relief), and interior partitions.

Cast stone is generally unreinforced, whereas cast concrete (more commonly termed "precast concrete") includes steel mesh or rod reinforcing. Cast stone may be used in similar locations, except that it is used as a non-bearing face element, with the actual bearing lintel, usually steel or segmental brick arches, concealed behind.

GENERAL GUIDELINES

All metals are subject to physical deterioration and corrosion. Examples of the former are: abrasion (critical on metal flashings and valleys on slate roofs); creep (critical with sheet lead roofs); metal fatigue; fire; aging; overloading; and weathering.

Corrosion or oxidation is the major type of metal deterioration: it is seen in forms ranging from uniform attack to pitting and cracking. (See "Corrosion" in the Glossary for types.)

When repairing metalwork, consider these two general guides:

Shape and Form

The appearance of metalwork is affected by its shape (sheet, plate, rod, or bar), the method by which it was shaped (rolled, extruded, cast, forged, wrought, cut, or stamped), and its dimensions. All these factors should be considered when repairing metalwork. Rod stock in a metal grate, for example, should not be replaced with bar stock. Cast and wrought iron should be produced using the original techniques because modern production methods cannot duplicate the original appeance of the metalwork. Usually, matching metalwork will require a special order through a foundry.

Color and Patina

The color of alloy metals is affected by the percentages of constituent elements. Other influences on the color, as well as the patina (the surface appearance) of metals include weathering, cleaning cycles, and pollutants, which, over time, act on the original finish. This relationship is most noticeable in copper and brass where environmental factors can cause a complete change of color.

When exterior metalwork of any kind is partially replaced, it will take a year or more for the patina to weather to closely match the remaining original work. Mild acidic washes can be used to accelerate the weathering process, but they are not recommended because they might alter the natural weathering process, lengthening it or even preventing an exact match from developing.

METALS AND THEIR CARE

Brass/Bronze

Brass is an alloy of copper and zinc. Bronze is an alloy of copper and tin. Both resist industrial, rural, and marine atmospheres, and weak acids. Both have poor resistance to ammonia, ferric and ammonia compounds, and cyanides.

Both materials are used for ornamental purposes, where strength and corrosive resistance are required.

Fasteners: Brass fasteners should be used to seam all brass sheets and fittings. Seaming should be constructed with lead-tin soldering and silver alloy brazing. Arc welding for this purpose is possible but not recommended. Bronze fasteners should be used to seam bronze sheets and fittings.

Bright Finishes: Polished finishes are recommended on surfaces that are continually handled (e.g., doors, pushplates, handles, etc.), and should be free of protective coatings to permit frequent polishing.

Statuary dark finishes: An antique or dark finish can be created artificially by brushing on several applications of potassium sulphide solution until the surface is darker than required. The finish is then lightened by gentle rubbing with fine steel wool (No. 00-No. 000) or powdered pumice. The final finish is set with a coating of lemon oil, followed by vigorous rubbing with a soft cloth.

Aluminum

Aluminum is soft; lightweight; non-magnetic; and silver in color. It has a low melting point, and is high in thermal and electrical conductivity. It has a moderately high coefficient of expansion, and is easily worked.

It is used for: sheet roofing; roofing shingles; flashing; gutters and downspouts; copings; skylights; cresting and cornices; siding; corrugated siding; spandrels; mullions; windows; storefronts; marquees; facades; doors; hardware; fences; gates; lighting fixtures; grilles and railings; structural members; ventilators and ducts; and mesh and wirecloth.

Agents which actively attack aluminum include: alkalis; hydrochloric acid, formic acid, oxalic and trichloracetic acids; halogen acids, nitric and sulphuric acids; lead base paints; green or damp wood; wood preservatives which contain the above acids or sodium and potassium hydroxide solutions; lime mortar; Portland cement plaster; concrete; and chlorides; erosion caused by abrasions; fatigue.

Cleaning: To clean anodized aluminum, use a mild abrasive or detergent wax every one to six months to minimize further corrosion. If this treatment is neglected, deep pitting can occur, requiring the aluminum to be replaced, or sprayed with tinted coatings.

For unanodized, lacquered aluminum, every one to three years (for exterior material) and five to ten years (for interior material), remove the lacquer. Polish with oxalic acid, and remove scratches with emory paper. Then apply new lacquer.

Restoration of Finishes: Sandblasted aluminum should be sandblasted again. Satin or wire brush finishes should be brushed by hand with German silver wires and a finishing compound of ground pumice stone and water. Buffed or polished aluminum should be rubbed with pumice.

Protection: To protect and preserve finish aluminum, coat the material with lacquer (acrylic-based) or varnish, and oil it periodically (e.g., yearly application of kerosene). When contact of aluminum with dissimilar metals cannot be avoided, coating with bituminous paint may be employed to avoid corrosion by galvanic action.

Fasteners: Use only aluminum fasteners to fasten aluminum.

Erosion: This problem, especially in roof valleys and flashing, may be solved with paint. If erosion is extensive, the aluminum element must be replaced with a new element of a heavier gauge.

Fatigue: Fatigue can be minimized by providing adequate expansion joints and continuous support under aluminum elements.

Copper

Copper is ductile; malleable; easily worked; non-magnetic; bright reddish brown in color; high in electrical and thermal conductivity; and easily soldered.

Its uses are: roofing shingles; decorative details; spandrels; roof ridges; cresting; flashing; gutters; leaders, dormers; cornices; plumbing pipes; exterior sheathing; hardware; weather stripping; screening; vents; wall tiles; anchors; screws; nuts; bolts; mesh wire and cloth; and lighting fixtures.

Copper is corroded by sulphur; sulphur trioxide can unite with water to form sulphuric acid which is very destructive. (Hydrogen sulfide and sulphur dioxide cause the formation of the green patina of exposed copper which acts as a protective coating against further corrosion.)

Alkalis can also corrode copper; ammonia causes stress, corrosion, cracking. Other corrosion factors are: carbon monoxide; combustion gases; illuminating gas; erosion and fatigue.

Fasteners: Copper should be fastened only with copper or bronze nails and clips.

Protection: Exposed copper oxidizes and forms a patina which acts as a shield against further deterioration. To prevent copper from tarnishing or forming a patina, the International Copper Research Association recommends the application of an inorganic undercoating, followed by a clear protective coating of polyvinyl fluoride.

Where water runoff from new copper could stain surfaces, the copper should be lead-coated. The lead coating cannot be applied to old copper in place. Where existing copper is staining and defacing surrounding materials, it may be painted. A new, clear coating called "Incralac" has been developed by the Copper Research Association to protect copper sheeting.

Tin

Cleaning: To remove the patina from copper, use chemical compounds such as rottenstone and oil, whiting and ammonia, or precipitated chalk and ammonia with very mild abrasive techniques such as rubbing with a clean, soft cloth. Steel wool and harsher abrasives should never be used. Once cleaned, the copper can then be coated with a clear lacquer or "Incralac" to prevent further corrosion.

Light tarnishing can be removed with commercial copper cleaner-polish.

Tin is soft; ductile; malleable; and bluish-white in color.

It is used as a: protective coating for iron or steel sheets; coating of pure tin is a "tinplate" or "bright tin." A coating of lead (75-90%) and tin (10-25%) is "terneplate" or "leaded tin;" tin is also used for roofing pans; flashing; gutters; downspouts; rainwater heads; and interior wall and ceiling sheathing.

When exposed to low temperatures for long periods of time, tin deteriorates by disintegrating and crumbling to a grey powder, called "tin pest" or "tin plaque." Usually this condition is not a problem with tin plate or terneplate used in architecture.

Tin is attacked by: acids and acid salts in the presence of oxygen; marine atmospheres; and alkalines.

Tin is normally covered by a thin film of stormic oxide which resists corrosion by oxygen, moisture, sulphur dioxide, and hydrogen sulfide.

Both sides of tin plate should be coated with a prime coat of linseed oil, and finish coats or a lacquer containing silicone or acrylic resin. External painting should be reviewed every few years to keep the metal from corroding.

Tar or bituminous compounds should never be used to coat or patch a tin or terneplate roof.

Lead

Lead is soft, and heavy in weight; blue-gray in color; easily recovered from scrap materials; relatively impenetrable to radiation; and toxic. It has a high coefficient of thermal expansion and resists corrosion by most acids or atmospheric corrosion.

It is used for: roofing; decorative spandrels; gutters; leader heads; downspouts; cupolas; spires; window mullions; vibration insulation pads in foundations; radiation insulation; piping; protective coating on sheet copper and sheet iron-terneplate (in combination with tin).

Lead is attacked by: acids (hydrochloric, hydrofluoric, acetic, formic and nitric); alkalis (lead should not be placed in contact with lime mortar, Portland cement or uncured concrete); lower fatty acids (given off by wood, varnish, plastic); tannic acid (from contact with oak); radiation (forms nitric acid which attacks the lead); erosion; and creep.

Erosion/Abrasion: Lead roof flashings and valleys can be protected by the application of paint and, if damaged, can be repaired by lead burning. Extensive damage requires that they be removed and replaced with new lead of heavier weight; they should not be patched by soldering or with asphalt or bituminous compounds.

Creep: Any lead sheet so damaged must be removed and replaced by a thicker sheet.

Fasteners: All fasteners to lead should be lead coated; cadmium nails are used with lead to avoid corrosion.

Cleaning: Clean with soap and water, using a soft cloth; protective films should not be removed.

Structural Steel

Steel is tough and malleable. Allowable working stresses for structural grade steel since 1900 have exceeded 30,000 psi (generally 30 ksi to 36 ksi), making it the strongest common building material available.

It is widely used in one form or other in most buildings built after 1890. (Metal members encountered in earlier buildings are probably wrought iron or cast iron.)

If the profile of a steel section can be measured accurately, the section properties, and therefore its load carrying capacity, can be quickly determined. The most useful reference in this regard is *Iron and Steel Beams 1873-1952,* published by the American Institute of Steel Construction, listing all the steel and wrought iron beams rolled in the United States. The manual is cross-referenced by manufacturer, year first rolled and cross sectional dimensions.

Cast Iron

Widely used in later nineteenth century construction, both structurally and decoratively, cast iron is frequently encountered in GSA's historic buildings.

It was used as: structural members, (columns, beams, built-up girders, trusses, dome framing); entire facades; roofing slabs; decorative roofing details and crestings; roof ridges; gutters; downspouts; doors; window and door shutters; cornices; railings and grilles; balustrades, stairway brackets; pipes and fittings; fences and gates; benches; plumbing fixtures; and hardware.

Caution: Do not increase or otherwise alter the loads imposed on cast iron members used structurally without consulting a qualified professional engineer, and after suitable analysis and testing.

77

Wrought Iron

Wrought iron was used for supporting beams in structures constructed from 1875-1890. Almost pure iron, it is often found in conjunction with cast iron columns or with brick or terra cotta floor arch construction. If the depth of the beam can be measured and it turns out to be 7 or 10-1/2 inches, it is probably wrought-iron. If the depth is greater than 15 inches, it must be steel because wrought-iron beams of that size were not rolled. The publication *Iron and Steel Beams 1873-1952* published by the AISC contains descriptions of the beams and columns rolled in the United States. A comparison of the physical dimensions, the manufacturer, and the year may be enought to categorically differentiate between wrought iron and steel. A more positive test is to apply a little dilute nitric acid to a thoroughly cleansed section of the beam. If the beam is wrought iron, it will not be affected: steel will turn black under the acid.

Wrought iron rusts more quickly than cast iron; it is resistant to progressive corrosion.

Wrought iron was used for: structural members; sheathing; roof sheeting; roofing plates (either tin-plate or terneplate); pipes; chains; grilles; railings; fences; screens; balustrades; and decorative objects.

The problems of wrought iron beams involve corrosion, fatigue, failure of connections, fire damage, overloading, and unauthorized alterations; they are similar to those of structural steel. Because wrought iron beams have a substantially lower safe-load capacity than comparably sized steel beams and may be weakened by the excessive heat of welding, overloading such a beam can result in a sudden catastrophic collapse.

Wood is subject to decay that leads to structural disintegration and destruction. Fire is the ultimate destructive force, but other causes of disintegration include thermal decay, hydrolysis, oxidation caused by ultra-violet light, rot, fungi and insects. "Weathering," or alternate swelling and shrinking, can have a major deteriorating effect. Each of these processes and combinations thereof cause the ultimate failure of wood.

MAINTENANCE AND REPAIR GUIDELINES

Protect against Rain Seepage

Sufficient overhangs at the eaves and gables are the most effective protection against rain seepage. Therefore, gutters, downspouts, and flashing should be frequently inspected and repaired as should joints, step rails, sloping treads, and sloping arches. Where overhangs are insufficient, consider alterations to flashing and gutters to help retard seepage.

Select Decay-Resistant Wood

(See Table 1 of Principles for Protecting Wood Buildings from Decay, USDA Forest Service Research Paper, FPL 190, 1973, p.5.)

Protect Exterior Wood from Water

Use dry uninfested lumber; protect stored lumber; use preservatives, water-repellents, tight joints, paint and non-shrinking caulk; divert water from joints; assure proper drainage; provide flashing to prevent water from entering critical junctures of the exterior; treat all exterior wood with water repellents (unless the wall contains no vapor barrier); install vapor barrier when possible; maintain good paint coatings on exterior wood.

Prevent Decay

Select decay-resistant heartwoods or treated woods for replacements (all replacements should be pressure-treated with preservatives and with water repellents, if necessary); investigate immediately the source of any dampness; regularly inspect water drainage systems (e.g., gutters, downspouts) to insure that they are functioning properly; do not allow soil to rise above the level of the damp-proof course; keep crawl space vents open; if flooding has occurred, remove the floor coverings and take up the floor boards along the outside walls; never use unseasoned or decay-infested timber in building.

FIRE RETARDANTS

Impregnating wood with fire retardants only moderately increases the wood's fire resistance. However, such treatments do reduce the tendency of wood to support combustion and to spread flame. Polyethylene glycol reduces the charring rate to a greater extent than any other chemical, but a mixture of borax and boric acid is most effective in checking the flaming and glow.

WOOD ADHESIVES AND FILLERS

For general purposes, a proper adhesive for wood will provide maximum strength and durability without resulting in longer range complications. Calcium caseinate is powerful and has been used for centuries. When mixed with a hardener, modern synthetic resins set by chemical action, but most of them shrink as they set. Epoxy resins, on the other hand, resist shrinkage. Various combinations of resins and hardeners are available and manufacturer's directions should be followed closely.

For filling irregular cavities Aerolite 300, a urea formaldehyde resin, is most satisfactory in providing strength. If a hole merely has to be filled, Bondafiller, glue and sawdust, or balsa wood inserts may be sufficient. Be sure to trim the filler after it has set.

WOOD PRESERVATIVES

There is a wide variety of wood preservatives. Although most new lumber has been pressure-treated with preservatives, old wood may never have been treated or may be in need of new treatment. There are a number of on-site, in-place treatments, and of these, pentachlorophenol in various solvents is widely applicable. (For information on wood preservative treatments, see Tables 4, 5 and 6 of "Principles for Protecting Wood Buildings from Decay," USDA, FPL 190, 1973.)

Pentachlorophenol Solutions

For general exterior wood treatment a 5 per cent pentachlorophenol solution in water should be applied to sanded wood before repainting. A 10 per cent solution may be desired for wood that is frequently wet. For waterproofing, a 20 per cent solution in water with oil or liquid paraffin additives is suggested. This mixture is especially useful at butt joints, end joints, or any vertical joints where gravity water flow could find easy access to wood members.

Dipping and Short Period Soaking

Dipping and short period soaking is effective if wood members are detachable. It can be done on site with a water repellent pentachlorophenol solution. (See Federal Specification TT-W-572.) The soaking period should be no less than three minutes, although longer treatments may be required for elements subjected to constant moisture. Wood should be submerged in the solution during treatment.

Penta-Grease Treating

Penta-grease penetrates more deeply than any other in-place surface preservative treatment. It is used chiefly on butt, end, and other vertical joints susceptible to the direct gravity flow of water, on wood subject to such moisture, or on wood whose water content does not easily evaporate. The penta-grease is thickly spread on the sanded raw wood. Complete absorption ceases when the layer of grease stops shrinking, a process which may take several days. After a waiting period of several weeks, the surfaces can be coated with an oil-based paint.

Flooding

In preparing the surface of exterior wood for repainting, enough time should be allowed for repeated flooding by preservative solutions as described above. All joints and openings should be cleaned mechanically of debris and old paint to allow maximum penetration.

Sterilization Treatment

Rot, in its advanced stages, deteriorates structural wood to the point where much of it must be replaced. By destroying the fungi, however, it may be possible to salvage some decorative feature or unique historic construction system. Sterilization is accomplished by heating moist wood in a kiln to a temperature of 150 degrees Fahrenheit (65 degrees Centigrade) for one hour per inch of thickness, maintaining high humidity to prevent surface drying and checking. A five-hour treatment, for example, would sterilize a member 4 x 4 inches.

Safety Precautions for Wood Preservative Treatments

1. Do not breathe dust or sprays or let them contact the face.

2. Protective gloves and aprons should be worn when handling wet lumber.

3. Wash the inside of gloves frequently.

4. Wash skin areas touched by preservatives with soap and water immediately.

5. Workmen with extreme skin sensitivity to preservatives should not be allowed on the site.

6. Consult federal, state and local authorities for possible prohibitions against, or warnings about, the preservative under consideration.

CRITERIA FOR MATCHING WOOD

Species

In matching unpainted wood, it is essential to obtain the same species.

Cut

The choice of cut can emphasize or deemphasize graining and, for this reason, it should be taken into account for the final match.

Dimensions of Finish Pieces

Often the original woodwork is not the size of standard lumber and finish wood trim available today; therefore, standard sizes must be cut down to match the original exactly. This process is time consuming and more expensive than using stock pieces, but it is necessary because small variations from the original trim are visually obvious and must be avoided.

Molding and Profiles

Presently there are only two methods of obtaining adequate and correct reproductions of original moldings:

a. **Recarving:** More and more craftsmen are training in such work, and the best of them are capable of recreating complex molding in the original fashion at a cost competitive with fiberglass reproduction.

b. **Fiberglass reproduction:** Provided that enough original molding still is available to create a new master mold, it is relatively easy and inexpensive to exactly reproduce the molding in fiberglass. The final appearance of fiberglass molding is indistinguishable from the original, if painted. (Because Victorian woodwork was usually left natural, it cannot be reproduced in fiberglass.)

Finish and Final Color

Finish and final color are most critical to a proper match of wood. Since finish coatings are subject to periodic renewal because of their limited lifespan, evidence of the original coating can be found only by laboratory analysis.

DETECTING AND CORRECTING DETERIORATION

Rot

Rot is detected by: discoloration (dark or light) in patches or streaks along the grain; loss of strength/weight; odor (fungal); more rapid water absorption; more rapid ignition, but smoldering; susceptibility to woodboring insects (hardwoods); easy penetration of a pen knife blade, but inability to raise a splinter; and fungus bodies.

The source of excess moisture should be removed. The wood should then be dried and brushed clean. A fungicide should be applied according to standard practice. (Sometimes, sterilization may be required, followed with a wood preservative treatment. Sterilization is unnecessary in treating wet rot.) Replace damaged wood with treated heartwood lumber.

White Rot: Wood darkens first, then becomes very light in color.

Brown Rot: Wood turns dark brown, and in final stages of decay, cracks along the grain, breaking into small, rectangular pieces.

Wet Rot: Microscopic fungal strands.

Dry Rot: Visible strands or growths.

Soft Rot: When dry, appears black and scaly.

Weathering

Produces discoloration; erosion; and disintegration.

Combat weathering forces with preservatives, water repellents, and proper paint coatings.

Insects

Drywood Termites: Difficult to detect; expert technical testing is required.

Fumigate the entire building with hydrogen cyanide or methyl bromide (treatment does not provide residual protection). Moveable components may be fumigated or dipped. For in-place elements, insecticides must be sprayed or pressure-injected through holes drilled at various intervals. Deodorized kerosene spray should be effective for in-place treatment. Once spraying is completed, holes should be plugged.

Caution: These treatments have adverse visual implications for historic structures and increase potential for fire damage. Consider the risk before proceeding.

Powder-Post Beetles: Detected by powder deposits beneath their exit holes. (Place a white cardboard under the suspected wood member and watch for powder accumulation.)

Preventative: Use a surface application of pentachlorophenol in a water-repellent solution.

Treatment: Use procedure described for drywood termites, although liquids are more potent against beetles.

A penta-grease application of heptachlor is also effective; apply with a trowel or caulking gun. (Members treated with grease are unpaintable.)

Previous paint should be removed before treatment.

If deodorized kerosene is used, wood should be allowed to dry for several days before being repainted with an oil-base paint. When painted or decoratively treated wood is required, small preliminary tests should be conducted and sufficient time should elapse to determine long-range effects.

Lyctus beetles have been effectively controlled for several years with a three-dip treatment of movable members with a 5 per cent pentachlorophenol or 2 per cent copper arsenate and a 9.25 per cent benzene hexachloride solution.

Anobiid Powder-Post Beetles: Detected by powder deposits beneath their exit holes.

Old House Borer: Detected by large elliptical adult emergence holes in coniferous wood.

Subterranean Termite: To prevent these termites poison the soil with chlordane, dieldrin, aldrin, or heptachlor emulsions. General site sanitation and chemical control should be supplemented with annual inspections. Termite shields are helpful, but do not prevent infestation.

Thermal Decay

Evident by loss of toughness, weight, and dimensional stability.

Hydrolysis

Wood, especially hardwood, loses strength.

Ultra-Violet Oxidation

Wood turns brown in dry conditions, or gray in humid conditions, depending on species.

Both lime and gypsum plaster or stucco are plastic enough to be shaped and molded when installed, yet they can become quite brittle. They are susceptible to the effects of moisture and chemical actions (especially efflorescence) common to masonry. Both are commonly whitewashed or painted. Properly maintained, they will last indefinitely.

CORRECTIVE MEASURES

Because plasters or stuccos, especially lime-based ones, are porous and generally of low density, they tend to deteriorate with age, especially if moisture is present. Deterioration is usually widespread within any particular structure. Attempts to make spot corrections are usually more costly and less satisfactory than removing the plaster and installing a new plaster system. Therefore, in most maintenance and repair work, a "repair vs. replace" decision frequently favors replacement.

In certain special cases, especially where the plaster finish or detail is too valuable or important to sacrifice, repair of failing plaster in situ is advisable. Plaster failure, revealed by looseness or separation, can result from rusting nails, decay of lath, or the breaking of the plaster "key" or the plaster between the laths. If plaster on ceilings or walls shows signs of failing or falling, it should be propped up immediately with planks and felt pads.

Before deciding on in-place repair, carefully evaluate the conditions. If possible, the ceiling or wall should be examined from above or behind. In either case, first clean away dust with soft brushes and a vacuum cleaner. In instances where such access is possible, a common repair method is backing plaster with new plaster. If you cannot get behind or above ornamental plaster, cut a test section for evaluation.

Re-bonding and/or consolidation treatments are sometimes successful. The choice of adhesives and bonding agents must be made after an evaluation of the chemical composition and condition of the plaster or stucco to be treated. Adhesive mixtures of casein, lime and polyvinyl acetate emulsion or of polyvinyl acetate with calcium carbonate additives have been used successfully. Consolidation treatments are similar to those processes used for stone; the problems of adverse chemical reactions and color changes may be more troublesome with plaster and stucco than with stone and brick, however. Both rebonding and consolidation techniques are complex and should be executed only by skilled technicians under the supervision of experienced professionals. Building Managers are encouraged to seek advice before proceeding with any undertaking of this nature.

REPAIRING PLASTER SURFACES

The discussion of specific problems, causes, and recommended corrective procedures which follows involves gypsum and lime plasters, cement plaster, and in certain situations, acoustical plaster. It is essential to identify and correct problems at their source before beginning corrective work on the material. The actual problem in the plaster may emanate from one or more sources. Wherever the word "improper" is indicated, the recommendations of the materials manufacturer and the standard specifications of the Gypsum Association for the particular work were not followed, thus creating the problem. It is essential that: 1) the backing for the plaster be in conformance with the requirements of the manufacturer and of the Gypsum Association; and 2) that plaster be mixed and applied without deviation from recommended procedures.

Efflorescence

1. Ensure that the cause of the moisture in the back-up materials has been eliminated.

2. Remove all surface deposits on plaster with a dry brush, and wipe all affected areas with a damp cloth.

Check-cracks

1. In severe cases, where the finish has broken its bond with the basecoats and can be removed easily in dry chips, flake out all such chips from each check-cracked area. Bevel the edges of the sound finish plaster around the perimeter of each area and dry brush all surfaces to properly receive the new finish plaster patch. Apply the bonding agent to the existing basecoat plaster, including all the edges of the cut areas, and permit the agent to dry in accordance with the manufacturer's recommendations. Mix and apply the finish coat of patching plaster (either a standard plaster joint compound or a veneer plaster — see Table 3.5.1); press it tightly against the back-up coat to establish a bond; immediately apply an additional layer of patching plaster, from the same batch, following the same procedure, to fill the crack to the level of the undisturbed surrounding finish coat. When the patching plaster has stiffened, remove the trowel marks and other surface imperfections with light trowel pressure. For a dense, polished finish, water-trowel the surrounding finish, and for a texture finish, float the surface.

2. In cases where the finish is bonded tightly to the basecoat, lightly sand the affected area with No. 000 cloth, removing all raised edges. Wash, rinse, and permit it to dry. If painting is not intended, prepare a slurry of plaster joint compound, and apply it over the area to blend in with the surrounding finish. If the surface is to be painted, apply one coat of a primer-sealer compatible with the finish coats of paint intended to be used.

Large Cracks

1. Before beginning any corrective measures, cut the plaster in the area of one crack through its entire thickness to the backing material. Verify the backing material and its general condition. Establish the type and thickness of the original plaster.

2. Rake and undercut the plaster for its full thickness making the cut sufficiently wide (generally double the width of the crack) to properly receive the patching plaster. Drybrush all loose plaster from the cut. Mix and apply basecoats of patching plaster as follows.

   a. Masonry, gypsum tile, clay tile, or unperforated gypsum lath backing:

      Scratch and Brown (double back) Coats: one cubic foot of sand per 100 pounds of wood fibered gypsum plaster applied with sufficient pressure to form a good bond with the back-up, straightened to the true surface with a rod and darby, and left rough to receive the finish coat.

   b. Wood lath, metal lath, or perforated gypsum lath backing:
      Scratch Coat: neat wood fibered gypsum plaster applied with sufficient material and pressure to form good full keys on backing and then cross-raked.

      Brown Coat: one cubic foot of sand per 100 pounds of wood fibered gypsum plaster applied after the scratch coat has set, straightened to the true surface with a rod and darby, and left rough to receive finish coat.

3. If the existing plaster finish surrounding the cut is smooth, use either a lime putty-gypsum trowel finish or a prepared gypsum trowel finish. Where this finish is both smooth and extremely hard, use a Keene's cement-line putty finish. (Note that medium-hard Keene's cement-lime putty finish is harder than gypsum-lime putty trowel finish and that extra-hard Keene's cement-lime putty finish is the hardest of all finishes.) Mixing proportions of finish coats shall be as follows.

   a. **Lime putty-gypsum trowel finish:** one part, by volume, gauging plaster (calcined gypsum) to not more than four and one half parts by volume, of lime putty.

   b. **Prepared gypsum trowel finish:** mix with water to correct consistency, in accordance with the manufacturer's directions.

87

    c. **Medium hard Keene's cement-lime putty finish:** one 100 pound bag of Keene's cement to not more than 100 pounds of lime putty.

    d. **Extra hard Keene's cement-lime putty finish:** one 100 pound bag of Keene's cement to not more than 50 pounds of lime putty.

4. If the existing plaster finish surrounding the crack is textured or sand floated, use either a gypsum sand float finish, a prepared gypsum sand float finish, or a Keene's cement-lime putty sand float finish. Mixing proportions of finish coats shall be as follows:

    a. **Gypsum sand float finish:** one part of gypsum neat unfibered plaster to two parts sand, by weight.

    b. **Prepared gypsum sand float finish:** mix with water to correct consistency, in accordance with the manufacturer's directions.

    c. **Keene's cement-lime putty and float finish:** two parts of lime putty, one and one-half parts of Keene's cement, and four and one-half parts of sand, by volume.

5. Apply the finish coats to a partially dry basecoat or to a thoroughly dry basecoat which has been evenly wetted by brushing or spraying with water. Avoid excessive use of water in all types of finish coat plastering.

    a. **Trowel finishes:** apply the trowel finish coat over the basecoat, scratch it in thoroughly, and double back, filling in the crack to a true, even surface. General thickness shall be 1/16 to 1/8 inch. Allow the finish to dry a few minutes and then water-trowel it to a smooth, evenly dense surface, free from "cat faces" and other blemishes or irregularities.

    b. **Float finishes:** apply the float finish coat over basecoat, scratch it in thoroughly to a true, even surface. Float the surface with wood, carpet, cork, rubber, or other type floats to desired texture, free from slick spots or other blemishes.

REPAIRING ORNAMENTAL PLASTER WORK (MINOR)

Repair small nicks, gouges, and chips in the following manner:

1. Dry brush damaged area to remove all loose plaster particles. If the shape of the damaged area is not conducive to a good

mechanical bond (i.e., undercut or "V" shaped), trim the cut edges of area to a slight reverse bevel.

2. Apply one coat of high quality liquid bonding agent to all parts of damaged area, and permit it to dry.

3. Prepare a mixture of gypsum molding plaster and lime putty in equal parts (equivalent to 50 pounds dry hydrated lime and 100 pounds of molding plaster), and apply it to the damaged area in one operation. Shape the mixture to surrounding profile, using moistened paper or cloth, to obtain a smooth dense finish. When the plaster is thoroughly dry and cured, perform the final shaping with No. 000 grit damp emory cloth.

REPAIRING ORNAMENTAL PLASTER (MAJOR)

Repair major damage to ornamental plaster in the following manner:

1. Undercut all the edges of the damaged area to the back-up material or base. If the back-up has been damaged, replace the metal lath, wood lath, or gypsum lath, as applicable, with new material. Patch damaged concrete and masonry back-up with patching cement, and permit patching to fully cure before proceeding with plaster work.

2. Apply one coat of high-quality liquid bonding agent to all solid back-up of concrete and masonry, and permit it to dry.

3. Mix and apply scratch and brown coats as previously described.

4. Prepare running and/or casting molds, as required for the condition, for cornice, rails, ribs, molding, or any condition which can be run in place. Use casting molds for additional ornamentation that cannot be run in place. Erect substantial supports for molds as each segment of the work is performed.

5. Mix and place plaster-of-paris (calcined gypsum) or gypsum molding plaster, as required, to match surrounding ornamental plaster work, over partially dry brown coat or a thoroughly dry brown coat which has been dampened by brushing or spraying with water.

6. Leave the molds in position until the plaster has cured fully. Remove the molds carefully to prevent damaging the newly molded areas. Perform final shaping, if required, with No. 000 grit emory cloth.

REPAIRING ACOUSTICAL PLASTER

Repair major and minor damage to acoustical plaster in the following manner:

1. If the basecoats have been damaged, undercut all the edges around the damaged area up to the back-up material or base. Dry-brush the damaged area clean. Mix and apply fibered gypsum scratch and brown coats, as previously specified for corrections in gypsum plaster work. Permit these coats to cure to a "green" state before continuing with the acoustical plaster work.

2. If the basecoats have not been damaged, undercut the acoustical plaster to its full thickness around the damaged area. Dry brush the damaged area clean.

3. Add water to high quality premixed acoustical plaster and machine mix (hand mixing is acceptable for small applications) in strict accordance with the manufacturer's recommendations.

4. Verify the need for primer with the manufacturer and, if such primer is required, apply it according to the manufacturer's recommendation.

5. Depending on the total thickness of the existing acoustical plaster surrounding the damaged area, scratch in a first coat of acoustical plaster, 3/8 inch to 7/16 inch thick, and darby it to a true, uniform, roughened surface, approximately 1/8 inch below the surrounding surface. Allow it to dry overnight.

6. Apply the finish coat, 1/8 inch thick, working from the wet edge to avoid joining marks. After this finish coat has hardened sufficiently, stipple, stipple-perforate, float, darby or trowel it to match the existing surrounding finish.

REPAIRING CEMENT PLASTER WORK

Repair major and minor damage to interior and exterior cement plaster (stucco) in the following manner:

1. For sound cement plaster, having small cracks or other cosmetic blemishes, clean the entire surface of the existing plaster with detergent, and rinse it with clear water. If the surface has been painted, remove paint by wire brushing. In some cases, where one or two coats of paint have been applied and are in a sound condition, it may not be necessary to completely remove the existing paint. In such cases, after washing and rinsing the surface apply one coat of high-quality liquid

bonding agent. Apply an overcoating (single finish coat) of new premixed Portland cement stucco to a thickness of approximately 1/8 inch, and texture it with a float faced with rubber, plastic foam, carpet, or other soft material, as required to achieve the desired face effect. Moist-cure the finish with fog spray until proper hydration takes place. Take special precautions to ensure that the temperature of the material is maintained at 50 degrees Fahrenheit during, and for not less than, 48 hours after application.

2. For unsound cement plaster, where segments have become detached from back-up base, remove all unsound areas, and verify the condition of the back-up or the base. Replace the damaged lath or any lath without sufficient mechanical bond with new self-furring galvanized metal lath. If the back-up is concrete or masonry, clean it completely of old cement plaster and apply one coat of high-quality liquid bonding agent. In cases where the unsound plaster cannot be removed from the backing or base, cover the entire surface with waterproof paper-backed, self-furring galvanized metal lath (wire fabric) or a combination of waterproof building paper or roofing felt and galvanized wire fabric lath.

After the surface has been properly prepared by any of the previously mentioned methods, prepare scratch coat mix of one part Portland cement to not less than three, nor more than five parts damp loose sand, by volume. Hydrated lime may be added to the mix, as a plasticizer, in an amount not exceeding 10 per cent (by weight) of Portland cement or 25 per cent (by volume). Apply the scratch coat to the back-up or base to a thickness of approximately 1/2 inch, covering all metal reinforcement. Scratch it horizontally for proper bond with brown coat. If the backup is concrete, masonry or other solid material, the scratch/double back brown coat method may be used. After the scratch coat on the metal lath has hardened enough to sustain the weight of both coats, evenly dampen the scratch coat with a fog spray and apply brown coat of the same mix to a thickness of approximately 3/8 inch, using a straight edge to bring it to a true plane surface. Remove deep scratches or surface defects in the brown coat before it hardens. Float the entire surface of the brown coat. Moist-cure the brown coat for at least 48 hours, and permit it to dry for at least five days before applying the finish coat.

Just prior to applying the finish coat, uniformly dampen the brown coat by fog spray. Mix the finish coat of cement plaster in accordance with the manufacturer's recommendations, and apply it over the brown coat to a thickness of approximately 1/8 inch. Texture, cure, and protect the finish coat as previously described for the overcoated method.

3. For large cracks in cement plaster, undercut all edges on both sides of the cracks to the back-up material or base. Dry brush the cracks clean. Apply one coat of high-quality liquid bonding agent to all surfaces of the damaged area. Mix and apply the scratch, brown, and finish coats as previously described.

CLEANING PLASTER AND STUCCO

Plaster and stucco may be cleaned by applying either temporary porous absorptive surface treatments or jellies of starch, methyl cellulose and water. These jellies should be spread on the surface and mechanically removed after drying.

Diluted ammonia may be used to remove mold and algae, but the type of infection should be identified conclusively to determine proper treatment.

As a durable exterior material, stucco in good condition can be cleaned by many of the gentler methods discussed in Section 3.1.4 Masonry Cleaning; **abrasive mechanical methods or wetting for extended periods of time should be avoided.** In most instances, repainting of soiled stucco is the easiest and most satisfactory course.

Table 3.5.1
Plaster Mix Recommendations

Base	Mix Proportions (by Volume) (Cement:lime:sand)		
	Scratch	Brown	Finish
Low absorption, i.e., dense concrete, claybrick, etc.	1:½:4—6	1:1:6—8	1:2:6—10
High absorption, i.e., concrete masonry porous clay brick	1:1:6—8	1:1:6—8	1:2:6—10
Metal lath or reinforcement	1:1:6—8	1:1:6—8	1:2:6—10

Note: Successive coats should never be stronger than the coat to which they are applied.
From: National Lime Association

Although sealants are a product of contemporary construction technology, they are used extensively in older buildings. Properly used, sealants can outperform any original joint closure technique found in such structures, offering a solution to the common preservation maintenance problem of water penetration at joints.

Caution: do not let the capability of sealants delude you into treating the symptom of joint failure or cracking without careful consideration and possible treatment of the cause of such failures as well.

PROPERTIES AND CHARACTERISTICS

Although different sealants may have similar physical properties, few are "equal" in performance under given circumstances. One major difference among sealants is their ability to withstand joint movement for indefinite periods of time (i.e., contraction without squeeze-out and elongation without adhesive or cohesive failure). Joints subject to "dynamic movement" receive the impact of frequent major movement ranging from 25 to 100 per cent of the original joint width. This movement may be caused by thermal effects on surrounding materials, or by volumetric changes such as wet-dry cycles, dynamic loading on horizontal surfaces, and uneven settlement in buildings. It is also quite possible that the original function of any joint can change because of environmental changes. (See Table 3.6.1)

Modern sealants are designed to perform various particular functions required by joint design. A twenty-year life span is minimal for most sealants formulated to accommodate dynamic movement. Certain sealants which are lower in cost and less sophisticated than those recommended here will perform the required function, but they have a reduced effective life span. Frequent replacement costs more than offset the single cost of a more expensive, longer-lasting material.

CORRECTIVE MEASURES

Unless the problem is an isolated condition, which can be remedied without disturbing the remaining sealant in the joint, completely remove the sealant and joint back-up material from problem joints.

Thoroughly clean the joint of the existing sealant and joint back-up material, using solvents and/or cleaners specifically recommended by the manufacturer of the sealant that will be used in correcting the joint condition.

After the joint has been cleaned, protect it with a non-contaminating covering to ensure that it will remain absolutely dry and dirt-free until replacement of the sealant. Verify all protective procedures and materials used with the sealant manufacturer, and follow all additional recommendations.

Three joint types are common to historic buildings and replacement of sealant and back-up joint bead in such cases shall be as follows.

Exterior above-grade vertical expansion joint, width generally between 3/4 and 2 inches, subject to dynamic movement:

1. Completely prime joint, in accordance with the sealant manufacturer's recommendations.

2. Insert into the joint a continuous closed cell polyethelene foam, or butyl rod, having a diameter 30 per cent larger than the joint width. Maintain a uniform distance of approximately 1/2 the joint width from the outer surface of the joint to the nearest surface of the back-up, but in no case greater than 5/8 of an inch nor less than 3/8 of an inch. Ensure that the back-up surface is wrinkle-free for the full height of the joint.

3. Apply non-staining masking tape or other masking material to wall faces on each side of the joint to prevent staining of the adjacent surfaces.

4. For joints up to and including 1 inch in width, use either a two-part polysulfide sealant (non-sagging), a two-part polyurethane sealant (non-sagging), or a silicone-base sealant (non-sagging) designed specifically for dynamic joint function. Follow the specific application and curing recommendations of the manufacturer. In general, the thickness of the sealant at the centerline of the joint shall be one half the joint width, but under no circumstances shall the sealant thickness be less than 1/4 of an inch or more than 1/2 of an inch. Maintain a distance of approximately 1/8 of an inch from the wall face back to the closest point of the sealant face.

5. Immediately after applying the sealant, tool the surface until it is uniformly dense, smooth, and free from bubbles and sagging. Use only water for tool wetting, if required.

6. For joints in excess of 1 inch in width but not more than 1-1/2 inches, use either a two-part polysulfide sealant (non-sagging) or two-part polytremdyne sealant. For joints be- 1-1/2 and 2 inches in width use only a two-part polytremdyne sealant. Install sealant in joints having widths of from 1 to 2 inches in the same manner specified for smaller joints, but place a continuous temporary dam, faced with a non-contaminating release agent (wood strip covered with waxed paper) over the large joints immediately after installing the

sealant. Leave it in place until the initial curing has taken place. Remove the temporary dam after sealant has set.

Joint Type 2

Exterior above-grade vertical and horizontal control or construction joint, width generally between 1/4 and 5/8 of an inch, subject to minimal movement:

Apply primer, back-up, and follow installation procedures previously specified for Joint Type 1, but use either one part polysulfide sealant (non-sagging), one part acrylic polymer sealant, silicone polymeric sealant, or one part hypalon sealant.

Joint Type 3

Exterior above-grade control or slip joint in metal-to-metal flashing connection:

1. Clean both surfaces of the metal completely free of solder, plastic cement, and other foreign matter. Use a film-free solvent to remove all oily residue, and follow with a detergent wash and clear rinse. Permit the surfaces to fully dry.

2. Completely prime the joint in accordance with the sealant manufacturer's recommendations.

3. Use either one part acrylic polymer sealant, one part polysulfide sealant (non-sagging), or silicone rubber base sealant.

4. Separate the joint between adjacent pieces of metal to approximately 1/4 of an inch to permit proper penetration of sealant into the joint. Apply the sealant with appropriate-sized nozzle on gun or tube, so that sealant penetrates at least 3/4 of an inch into the joint. Tool sealant surface until it is uniformly dense and free from bubbles and from sagging.

SPECIAL CONDITIONS AND PRE-CAUTIONS

A thorough inspection for causes of sealant failures should include not only visually apparent conditions, but also such possibilities as previous use of chemical cleaners for other surfaces in the immediate area; masonry and stone sealers; wash-offs from treated wood; and water-borne acids transmitted from live growth on other surfaces such as roofs. In addition, under certain circumstances, some sealants (such as "butyl-based sealants" or "urethane-based sealants"), contain other materials in varying amounts which can change the performance characteristics and effective lifespan of the sealant. All performance and test data must be obtained from the manufacturer before beginning any sealant replacement work; this data should determine the limitations of the particular materials to be used.

Do not use oleo-resinous caulking material for sealing joints in natural-finished woodwork or between natural-finished wood and dissimilar material. Such caulking material can bleed into the wood because of its oil base.

If replacement sealant is to be painted, check the properties of the particular sealant for the length of time required for "skinning" sufficiently to receive paint. Use only the type of paint recommended by the sealant manufacturer to prevent damage to the sealant and to ensure proper paint adhesion.

Do not install sealant in any joint directly adjacent to materials that have not been permitted to fully cure.

Sealants are frequently and mistakenly used in lieu of mortar joints across the entire masonry surfaces (especially stone walls), rather than just in the limited cases where moving joints are encountered. This technique is ill-advised, because sealant characteristics (e.g., flexibility, limited life, high cost, inability to sustain loads) are far from what is desired of a good mortar (e.g., rigidity, long life, low cost, load bearing). **Substitution of sealants for mortar is strongly discouraged.**

Table 3.6.1
Causes of Common Sealant Problems

	Disintegrate	Sagging (vert.)	Bond failure	Tearing	Bleeding	Bulging	Softness
Improper material for joint function	●	●	●		●		●
Age beyond original life expectancy	●						
Ultra-violet reaction over years	●						
Chemical breakdown (atmosphere) (non-compatible finish)	●				●		●
Migration of incompatible adjacent or back-up material into sealant	●	●	●				
Joint width or movement in excess of maximum recommended for sealant		●		●			
Improper width-to-depth ratio for sealant used		●		●			
Improper mixing of multi-component sealant		●	●				●
Periodic temperatures in excess of those recommended for sealant		●	●				
Improper joint preparation			●				
High internal stresses in sealant, increasing with age — adhesion loss			●				
Age-hardening of release-type sealant reducing ability to move with joint			●	●			
Outward displacement of sealant from a non-resilient material resisting compression as changes occur in joint						●	
Pump-out of sealant from heat build-up						●	
Normal condition of sealant when joint is in compressed position and therefore not considered a problem						●	

MATCHING PAINTS AND PAINT COLORS

In older buildings, it is unlikely that original painted surfaces have survived in restorable condition; therefore, these guidelines will deal with sympathetic treatments using contemporary materials.

It is always safest to recoat surfaces with the same kind of paint previously used. The entire coating system must be compatible through each layer, from substrate to surface, to achieve optimum durability. Any incompatibility between substrate and paint system, and between coats, will reduce adhesion and accelerate deterioration.

Until the 1950's and the advent of "latex" paints, the common coating for wood surfaces was oil-based paint largely consisting of lead or zinc white.

Modern synthetic pigments are stable substitutes for most early pigments. However, because of the complexity of such judgments, the determination of original paint colors and the process of matching new paint in distinguished spaces should be undertaken by a professional with the technical equipment and knowledge of current research in historic paint and pigments. In less significant rooms, a visual match is probably sufficient, provided that color chips of four or five of the major paint manufacturers are reviewed for the closest match. Since some paint chips are very poor representations of the actual color, it is recommended that a small quantity, a quart or less, be used on a large sample panel adjacent to the test patch for comparison. Original paint type and color should be coded to a present universal standard so that the closest possible color and texture will result.

Refer to the following documents for further general information about paint and painting:

GSA Guide Specification No. 4-0990.01, January, 1969, including Amendments Nos. 1-3

GSA Tentative Guide Specification No. T2-0990, April 1973

PBS Painting Program Recommendations (HB, Operation and Maintenance of Real Property, Chapter 15, PBS P5800.18A)

SURFACE PREPARATION FOR REPAINTING

Paint will not adhere, provide the required protection, or have the desired appearance when applied to an improperly prepared surface. This is especially important in exterior painting where environment can cause accelerated deterioration of the coating and substrate.

Surface preparation usually involves at least one of two activities: removal and cleaning.

Paint Removal

Two principal means of paint removal are used in historic buildings:

a. **Mechanical Treatment:** Use hand tools such as scrapers, fiber and wire brushes and sanding blocks.

For large areas, power tools such as rotary scalers, sanders or wire brushes may be more efficient, but also increase the possibility of accidental damage to the substrate.

The use of blast cleaning with abrasive grit is undesirable for both wood and masonry, but it is effective for ferrous metal surfaces of sufficient thickness.

b. **Chemical Paint Remover:** If chemical paint removers are utilized, extreme care should be taken to remove all chemicals from the cleaned surface. Failure to do so may cause damage to the new paint (especially in humid conditions and on porous wood surfaces).

Some removers contain paraffin wax, which must be removed entirely from the surface to allow adequate bonding of the new paint. Sand with fine paper or steel wool or clean with a solvent. If solvent is used, again make sure that all is removed before painting.

Cleaning

a. **Resin/Varnish on Unpainted Wood:** If varnished surface is in good condition, without large scratches, gouges, cracks, it can be cleaned with commercial wood cleaners such as "liquid gold" or turpentine, mineral spirits, or solvent naphtha and a soft, lint-free cloth.

If varnish has been damaged, the surface can be renewed by rubbing it with a fine grade steel wool (No. 1 or 0) dipped in anhydrous alcohol (a mild varnish solvent). This will not remove all of the varnish, but will partially dissolve and smooth the varnish coating while removing dirt. When the steel wool becomes clogged with old varnish, use a fresh piece. Avoid excessive quantities of alcohol or rubbing. Attempt to remove only the surface of the varnish.

b. **Resin/Varnish over Paint:** Use nonaqueous turpentine, mineral spirits or solvent naphtha applied sparingly with a soft, lint-free cloth. Extreme pressure and rubbing is not required.

Care must be taken if varnish is damaged, cracked, or chipped to not damage or remove the underlying paint.

c. **Oil Based Paint:** Use damp cloth and mild detergent; rinse. Avoid using large amounts of water which may penetrate the paint layer(s) and wet the substrate, causing bonding failure.

d. **Limewash, Distemper:** Limewash, distemper cannot be cleaned safely and effectively.

Well-dried tempera may be cleaned with acetone or anhydrous alcohol if applied very cautiously. Inexperienced persons should not attempt this.

e. **Painted Iron and Steel:** (Refer to discussion of cleaning and surface preparation later in this section.)

f. **Painted Non-Ferrous Metals:** Remove loose surface material by scraping and sanding carefully to avoid damage to substrate; feather edges all around exposed areas. Clean thoroughly of all dirt, oil and grease. Treat the exposed metal areas as in new work and spot prime.

Special Surface Conditions

a. **Chalking:** Sand surface to remove all loose material.

b. **Alligatoring:** Sand entire surface removing all of the damaged coating(s).

   Caution: Avoid wearing down surfaces of carved molding while sanding.

c. **Peeling:** Scrape/sand surface to remove loose material. Sand entire surface to remove all of the damaged coating(s), and feather edges of remaining paint.

d. **Blistering:** Determine source of moisture and correct. Scrape off loose surface material, sand entire surface, and prime bare places where substrate may be exposed.

e. **Checking:** Scrape/sand surface. Remove all damaged coatings down to a sound undercoating.

f. **Cracking:** Remove all paint layers to the substrate by scraping/sanding and feathering into undisturbed coating.

g. **Crawling:** Remove surface layers to sound undercoating by scraping/sanding/feathering.

h. **Inadequate Gloss:** Remove surface layers to sound undercoating by scraping/sanding.

i. **Wrinkling:** Remove surface coats to undamaged undercoats by sanding. Apply new coats thinly, carefully brushing out each coat.

j. **Bleeding:** Sand entire surface, seal areas of stain, and sand again.

k. **Mildew:** Scrub surface with trisodium phosphate solution (2 to 8 oz./gal. water) and a medium soft brush; rinse thoroughly. Wet all areas before applying, cleaning small areas at a time.

REPAINTING EXTERIOR WOOD

Before repainting, inspect wooden elements for deterioration, and replace excessively rotted, decayed, or faulty pieces. Loose boards should be fastened and nail heads sunk. Sand all painted surfaces to provide a smooth bonding surface. Cracks, checks and small splits should be cleaned out to good wood and sealed with a non-shrinking caulking compound. Fill or caulk joints abutting walls or any vertical gaps. Apply a penta-chlorophenol solution to the wood as a preservative. If the wall contains a vapor barrier, treat the entire surface. The wood should completely dry before painting. After staining, knots should be treated with knot sealers and fillers may be required to smooth the surface of porous hardwoods.

Paint when the temperature is between 45 degrees and 95 degrees Fahrenheit and the relative humidity is less than 60 per cent. Allow wood to completely dry after rain storms. Three coats of oil-based paint will usually provide durability and a cosmetic result similar to that of the original paint.

REPAINTING MASONRY

Remove old paint and patch all cracks, openings, and broken areas. Remove all loose mortar, stucco, plaster, etc., and make appropriate repairs. Thoroughly clean all surfaces. Remove efflorescence by dry brushing with a stiff non-ferrous brush. Dampen surfaces to receive cement-water paints within one hour; use hose or pressure tank sprayer (brush application is inadequate). Surface must be moist when paint is applied. Redampen as necessary as work progresses. (For latex paints, the surface need not be damp.)

REPAINTING IRON AND STEEL

Clean and prepare the surface in one of the following ways:

Flame Cleaning

An oxyacetylene flame, a series of small, closely spaced, very hot flames projected at a high velocity, is applied to the metal. This process reduces ordinary rust to iron oxide and pops off loose scale. After flame cleaning, the surface should be wirebrushed.

Iron Phosphate

The metal is immersed in an alkali precleaner and then in a patented solution containing ferric phosphate. This treatment retards rusting and provides an excellent surface for adhesion of paint.

Pickling (Phosphoric Acid)

The metal is immersed in warm dilute phosphoric acid with added rust inhibitors; it does not need finishing. This treatment removes all dirt, rust, and mill scale and gives the surface a protective film which retards rusting and provides a good base for painting.

Pickling (Sulphuric Acid)

The metal is immersed in a solution of warm dilute sulphuric acid and other retardant chemicals added to confine the action of the acid to the rust and scale; the metal then is rinsed. The process removes all dirt, rust, and mill scale and gives the surface a slight etching which helps paint adhere.

Rust Removers

Rust removers are applied by brush or spraying. The phosphate-type remover forms a film and retards rusting. Generally, it is used in maintenance painting and with on-site painting where slight rusting has occurred.

Sand and Grit Blasting

Sand or steel grit in a range of No.10 to 45 screen sizes is used with dry compressed air at 80 to 100 psi. The process removes all dirt, rust, mill scale, and all other surface impurities; it also roughens the surface to provide good paint adhesion.

Solvent Cleaning

The metal is wiped with turpentine or mineral spirits to remove all dirt, oil, and grease.

Wire Brushing

Wire brushes, operated either by hand or mechanically, are used to remove rust and loose mill scale; they will not remove tight scale or rust. Too much wire brushing gives a polished surface which has poor paint adhesion.

DECORATIVE TECHNIQUES

Surface Texture

Brush application creates "ropiness," an uneven surface and evident brush marks. Apply new paint intended to look old with brushes to create a similar texture.

Graining

Surfaces painted to imitate wood grain in both color and pattern are said to be "grained." The graining consists of three distinct paint coats:

a. **Base coat(s):** This coat is pigmented to match the lightest color of the wood grain being imitated. It may be done in oil or watercolor.

b. **Grain:** The grain can consist of one or many paint colors applied to the base coat in a wood grain pattern by allowing the base coat to show through in some areas. The paint is applied with brushes of varying sizes and sometimes with rubber combs specially designed for this purpose. Either oil or watercolor paint may be used. (The range of color depends on the wood grain being imitated.)

c. **Varnish/glaze coat(s):** The varnish is an oil-resin forming the finish coating or glaze for the graining, protecting it and providing gloss. It may be clear or pigmented slightly.

Marbling

Marbling is the painting of surfaces to imitate marble. It consists of three coats of paint:

a. **Base coat(s):** The base coat is pigmented to match the field color of the marble being imitated. It may be painted in oil or watercolor.

b. **Veining:** Veining is oil or watercolor paint applied over the base coat, with small brushes and feathers, to create the pattern of marble. It can be one or many colors depending on the marble being imitated.

c. **Varnish/glaze coat(s):** The varnish is an oil-resin forming the finish or glaze coat for the marbling, protecting it and providing gloss. It may be clear or pigmented.

Glazes

Glazes can constitute any paint layer, clear or pigmented, which, together with the base coat, form a single finish painted surface. The quantity of a glaze medium in relation to the quantity of pigment is quite high, forming a transparent film through which light is reflected from the surface beneath it.

UNCOVERING HISTORIC DECORATIVE PAINTING

It may be possible to remove paint layers covering significant decorative painting when it was: 1) exposed for an extended period of time before being painted over, allowing dirt deposits to form; or 2) varnished upon its completion. In both cases an imperfect bond is formed between the decorative layer and subsequent paint layers. Removal techniques include:

Mechanical Removal

Paint layers can be successfully removed with little damage to the decorative layers by careful scraping and lifting with a surgical scalpel. Sanding is not recommended.

Chemical Removal

Solvents must be chosen according to the paint film to be removed. Medium, pigments, age, and environmental conditions are all factors in choosing the correct solvent.

Uncovering of original decorative painting is a delicate and specialized skill; obtain expert advice prior to undertaking it.

Following are some of the structural conditions that you may encounter in older GSA buildings. Detection procedures and corrective guidelines are also given.

WOOD JOISTS AND BEAMS

Sagging at Center of Span

Investigative Procedures: Determine general arrangement of floor framing by: locating main bearing walls or beams and columns supporting each end of floor joists (often best accomplished by inspecting framing not covered by finishes in attic or basement); tracking these bearing lines up or down to problem level (measurements from fixed reference points common to each floor level, such as exterior walls or the edge of stair wells are often helpful in keeping track of the location of bearing lines); measuring the distance between lines of bearing.

Probable Cause: If the sag at the center of the span is greater than the span in inches divided by 40 (5/8 in. in 12 ft.), the floor is probably overloaded. If the sag does not lessen with removal of the load the wood may have developed permanent set from long-term dead loading or may have failed.

Remedy: If the sag does not noticeably lessen with removal of the load, inspect the joists for bending failure which can be seen by a long split in the wood starting at the bottom edge of the joist or beam in the center half of the span. If there is no failure in bending at the center or in shear near the end of the beam, gradual sagging is probably long term deformation. There is no remedy other than leveling the top floor surface with blocking.

Excessive Springiness or Vibration

Investigative Procedures: Determine general arrangement and bearing lines. Measure length of span and measure size and spacing of joists. Look for possible missing structural elements below walls or columns. Obvious indicators include: patched plaster areas in ceiling below; bearing wall or column above floor level with no corresponding wall or column below floor level.

Probable Cause: If joist spacing is excessive (over 24 in. o.c.), the floor boards spanning between joists may be too springy. Similarly if the span of narrow (2 in. wide) joists in inches divided by 18 is greater than the depth of joists (8 in. deep joists spanning greater than 12 ft.), the joists may be spanning too far for their depth and loading condition.

Removed structural element (wall or column) below floor usually causes sag and springiness of beam supporting ends of joists which makes the entire floor seem springy.

Remedy: If springiness is not related to overstressing or damage to framing, avoid using the space for occupanices which result in heavier traffic or loads, or reduce existing load and traffic. If heavier loads must be introduced, reinforce floor with additional framing.

If springiness is related to overstressing, damaged or removed supports, immediate removal of loads and reinforcement of framing is necessary.

Pronounced Slope in One Direction

Investigative Procedures: Determine general arrangement of framing and bearing lines, and the type of construction of bearing line (i.e., wood beams and columns, wood partitions, masonry walls, etc.); measure pitch at each floor level.

Probable Cause: If total amount of slope increases on upper stories relative to the lower stories (a situation which is very common), the pitch of the floor is probably caused by the shrinkage of wood timbers. This shrinkage is particularly noticeable where one end of a timber is supported on wooden partitions or on wood posts and beams, while the other end leans on masonry.

If all floors pitch uniformly and there are confirming cracks in masonry walls, plaster finishes, and foundations, the pitch of the floors is probably caused by foundation settlement.

Remedy: Correcting settling foundations usually involves a major engineering study and costly underpinning in order to stabilize the situation, not to redress it. Unless floor slopes in an historic building are so pronounced that they inhibit occupancy and safe movement, it is best to intervene only enough to arrest further settlement. Jacking up the floor to level may be costly and destructive to finishes while leveling the existing floors affects interior detail and adds unwelcome dead load; neither procedure is recommended.

Joist Failure

Remedy: If joists have failed totally, remove and replace them. If split at bottom, install new joists alongside and spike or bolt to the existing joists or reduce loading as necessary to the safe capacity of the reinforced floor. If a major beam has failed in shear, reinforce the end of the beam with steel plates and provide a saddle hanger to transfer the load at the connection.

Sagging Plaster Ceilings

Probable Cause: Loosening of whole wood suspension system (caused by drying lath, resultant shrinkage and loosening of nails, or excessive loading of new layers of plaster or plasterboard); or separation of wood lath from its supports or separation of plaster from lath (usually caused by water leakage or inadequate original nailing of lath, aggravated by shrinkage, vibration or deflection).

Remedy: Remove and replace, or repair, strengthen and reattach existing plaster.

Floor Squeaking

Probable Cause: Loosening of the nails in the subfloor, due to drying and shrinkage of the lumber; loosening of the nails in the finish treads of wooden stairs.

Remedy: Renail subfloor into joists through finish floor using special hardened screw nails or resin-coated nails. It is possible to glue subfloor to joists using new vinyl glues; however, this extensive and disruptive process requires removal and replacement of both the finish and subflooring. If the ceiling of the space below can be readily removed, nailing and/or gluing can be more easily accomplished.

Insect Infestation

(See Section 3.4)

UNIT MASONRY VAULTS

Weakened Arch Structure

Probable Cause: 1) Cutting or corrosion of steel tie rods; 2) Rusting of supporting steel beams (usually 4 to 8 feet on centers) which support brick arches; 3) Movement of supports for arched floor usually caused by settlement of vertical support members. (See Figures 4.1.1 and 4.1.2)

Remedy: Stop water infiltration if it is causing efflorescence, rusting of steel. Pressure grouting with various proprietary Portland cement and epoxy compounds has been effective in restoring the structural capacity of cracked masonry arches. Corroded steel supports can sometimes be repaired, strengthened or replaced without dismantling all of the masonry.

Temporary shoring to relieve the steel member concerned is required, as is the approval of a licensed structural engineer.

Such a system can be safely penetrated by small ducts, pipes or recessed lighting fixtures since the structure acts monolithically to support the punctured section of the arch. Holes cannot, however, normally exceed one foot in any dimension or be spaced closer than four feet on center. One or more complete arch units may be removed from between steel supports; each arch is independent of those adjacent to it. Steel can in no circumstance be cut or reduced in cross sectional area and may require stiffeners if arch unit removal is contemplated. All such work should be reviewed and approved by a licensed structural engineer before execution.

CAST IRON FLOOR SYSTEMS

Cracking;
Corrosion Deterioration

Investigative Procedures: Any observed shifting of cast iron columns or the beams connected to them or cracks observed in brackets, castings, or columns must be immediately reported to the Building Manager and then to a professional structural engineer.

Remedy: If the cracking or deterioration is severe, make immediate preparations to unload the area, shore the affected beams and replace the defective material. Cracks may be welded (essentially a filling operation which does not disturb the parent metal or deposit soft steel by electric arc welding); however, these procedures are complex and are not recommended unless a structural engineer and technical experts concur in the approach.

Under no circumstances should brackets or clips be field-welded, or drilled and bolted into existing cast iron columns to effect repairs or alterations. If such strengthening of existing columns or attachment to them is necessary, construct new steel columns alongside the existing cast iron column, or shore, remove and replace defective elements.

Surface corrosion and deterioration may be remedied by removing loose scale from the affected area, priming with zinc chromate and painting well with metal paint.

STEEL BEAMS AND COLUMNS

Anticipating Structural Failure

Symptoms; Investigative Procedures: Angle irons supporting exterior masonry may show streaks of rust staining; or the rust may have forced brick courses above the angle out of the plane of the wall; rust staining near the base of a steel column may indicate severe moisture exposure; excessive springiness, especially low cycle vibration of a heavily loaded floor, may indicate the floor is overloaded beyond its safe live-load capacity.

Steel columns and beams are commonly concealed by fireproofing, such as concrete encasement, or other finishes causing steel members to sometimes be mistaken for concrete beams and columns. To determine whether the system is reinforced concrete or structural steel, one must either have the original plans of the building or must remove a small amount of concrete from the bottom of a beam or a face of a column and expose either reinforcing bars of the reinforced concrete or flat plates of the structural steel.

If the sizes of the structural members are not recorded on original building plans, the determination of such sizes will require extensive removal of finishes and fireproofing. In most instances, the investigation of structural steel will occur only after the problem has become severe or after a local failure. It is the nature of steel to fail quickly without warning when ultimate loads are exceeded or when the material has been weakened by any of the following causes:

Rust or corrosion: Where basements extend under sidewalks and other areas below grade where steel framing is exposed to wear, salt or other corroding medium, steel will deteriorate gradually. In above-grade areas, rusting and corrosion can occur where repeated leakage or humid conditions exist.

Fatigue: Caused by repeated loading and unloading (e.g., from heavy vibrating mechanical equipment). This is not a common occurrence in building frames.

Overloading: Can easily result from changes in use (e.g., conversion of office space into a library), files piled too high in records storage areas (especially where high ceilings allow), the introduction of heavy equipment in an area for which it was not designed.

Bolt or rivet failures or omissions: Omissions of such fasteners, the result of carelessness during original construction or alterations, can result in failures from overstress, loosening, rusting, corrosion, etc.

Welding: Extensively used in recent steel construction or repair, welding can induce overstress, overheat and thus weaken the member or cause failures.

Cutting members during alterations: Generally, main beams and columns are regarded with respect by alteration crews, but bracing members and other secondary members are likely candidates for cutting or removal during installation of plumbing, mechanical ducts, equipment, etc.

Catastrophes: Fire, windstorm, earthquakes, floods and other disasters (i.e., explosions) can damage and overstress steel framing.

Remedy: All damage must be assessed and all repairs must be coordinated by a qualified registered engineer.

Do not overload floors beyond their safe load capacities. Use reason and caution when stacking records, expanding file and library areas, etc. Coordinate all major occupancy changes, renovations and expansions with an architect and a registered engineer.

Periodically inspect any unoccupied or inaccessible areas or areas of infrequent use for moisture or other corroding atmospheres. Eliminate any wet or otherwise hostile environments. Any damage to steel must be assessed by a registered engineer.

Carefully inspect all alterations to insure that main beams, columns and secondary framing members have not been left cut or weakened. All alterations of steel structural framing must be under the direction of a registered engineer.

Any structural steel member exposed to the effects of fire, especially if it has discolored or become mis-shapen should be promptly evaluated by a qualified engineer and testing laboratory.

REINFORCED CONCRETE
(Also refer to Guide Specifications FCGS 4-0330.)

Spalling

Investigative Procedures: GSA personnel should periodically conduct a visual inspection of reinforced concrete. If symptoms occur, a structural engineer and testing agency should be retained to undertake a detailed evaluation and testing program (e.g., cores, Swiss hammer tests, chemical evaluation, etc.).

Probable Cause: Efflorescence; anchor corrosion; dynamic movement; poor quality concrete mix or improper installation workmanship.

Remedy: Since the cause of spalling is usually related to water penetration, eliminate the source of the water leakage. Depending on the size and depth of the spall, the steel should be wire-brushed, coated with zinc-rich paint, the entire area liberally coated with a commercially available bonding agent and then parged with a stiff plaster mix of one part Portland cement and 2/5 parts fine sand. This patch must be kept moist for five days.

Rust Spots

Probable Cause: Corrosion of anchors and reinforcing due to water penetration.

Remedy: Expose rusted steel by removing friable material; treat reinforcing as for spalling.

Surface Cracks

Probable Cause: Similar to spalling above, or structural over-stress.

Remedy: Surface cracks can be repaired effectively by sand epoxy mixes to provide a patch stronger than the parent concrete. Detailed recommendations for use of epoxy repair methods are contained in the Report of ACI Committee 403, dated September 1962, entitled "Guide for Use of Epoxy Compounds with Concrete."

Cracked Structural Members

Probable Cause: Similar to spalling and surface cracks.

Remedy: Major structural repairs of cracked concrete beams, slabs or walls should be undertaken only after a thorough investigation by a structural engineer. All structural repairs on reinforced concrete loadbearing elements should be carried out under direct engineering supervision.

SOLID CAST GYPSUM SLABS

Cracking

Investigative Procedures: The closely-spaced cable reinforcing is easily exposed by chipping away the soft gypsum and wood chip cover.

Probable Cause: Since the cables are not bonded to the gypsum but act as catenaries, even minor holes made in the slab after the initial construction will seriously weaken local areas. While the gypsum acts very well as a fire barrier it loses its strength when exposed to water or dampness for prolonged periods. Sagging is also a problem.

Remedy: If new holes must be cut which result in cutting the cable reinforcing, it must be anchored at the cut to preserve its continuity which may extend over many spans. If the gypsum becomes water-logged and takes a permanent sag, the floor may be leveled with furring strips or leveling compound after the gypsum is thoroughly dry.

CINDER CONCRETE FLOOR SLABS

Weak, Friable Concrete

Probable Cause: The cinders contain sulfides and other chemicals which in the presence of moisture can corrode the structural steel and more importantly, the light wire mesh reinforcing.

Remedy: Because of the close beam spacing, it is relatively easy to reinforce new openings with steel and/or to cast new light weight concrete slabs on the steel frame as appropriate. Where the slab has cracked and the light mesh reinforcing has corroded, it is necessary to first eliminate the source of the moisture and to cut the slab back to sound concrete and steel.

COMPOSITE STEEL AND CONCRETE

There are seldom major structural problems unique to this type of framing itself.

Investigative Procedures: It may be difficult to differentiate between the system and a reinforced concrete frame because the steel frame is frequently encased with concrete or plaster. Since

111

roof trusses or beams were often not fireproofed, the easiest place to look for the exposed steel, and possibly the tops of columns, is in an attic or furred space below the roof. Frequently, small areas of the concrete encasement will be spalled in places in the basement mechanical areas, or base plates and clip angles at connections of columns and beams will not be fully encased. A projecting angle or solid plate is a good indication that the main framework is steel. There are a few hybrid systems that have frameworks partially constructed of structural reinforced concrete and structural steel, but they are unusual.

The thickness of the concrete floor systems can usually be determined by measuring through a hole for piping, but since larger openings were usually framed with beams, it is usually not sufficient to measure the slab thickness around stairs and larger duct shafts.

Since the span of simple concrete floors was traditionally limited to the slab thickness (in inches) times 30, the probable thickness can be quickly found if the pattern of beams is visible. For example, with beams at 10 feet on center, the thickness of the slab is probably: 10 (12)/39 = 4 inches thick. In this case, the main reinforcing steel runs in the short direction (10 feet), and modest sized openings 2 to 3 times the slab thickness present no problems. In other cases where the column layout produces square panels 16 to 25 feet on a side and there is no intermediate beam present, the floor system is probably a two-way flat slab. The pattern of reinforcing is more complicated and major holes which require cutting more than one or two reinforcing bars should not be done without a structural engineer's approval.

Remedy: Refer to sections on structural steel and reinforced concrete.

SPECIAL SYSTEMS: TIMBER ROOF TRUSSES

Sagging

Probable Cause: Often caused by shrinkage of heavy timber used to construct original trusses; overloading of attic joists and roof purlins as a result of new mechanical equipment or introduction of dead record storage in areas not specifically designed for heavy storage; loosening of bolts; cutting of members to accommodate airhandling ducts; decay of members, particularly where members are built into masonry wall, or at poorly ventilated eaves.

Local Failure

Probable Cause: Splitting at connections; brittle failure of bolts; failure of purlins or ceiling joists framing into truss. Failure of connections is often due to improper original construction—too little distance of wood from end or edge to the bolt. General sagging is often enough to drastically reduce bearing for roof purlins and ceiling joists supported on truss which leads to local distress or failure.

Remedy: Retain an experienced structural engineer to analyze truss if sagging occurred after the addition of mechanical equipment ducts or piping in attic. If decay is present in main members of truss, strengthen with wood or steel plates bolted on as necessary. Also, eliminate source of decay (probably due to roof leaks and poorly ventilated attic space). Purlins or attic floor joists with insufficient bearing can be properly attached to truss with saddle-type hangers or light steel framing anchors, depending on the load.

FIGURE 4.1.1
TYPICAL MASONRY VAULT AND COLUMNS, TIMBER TRUSSES

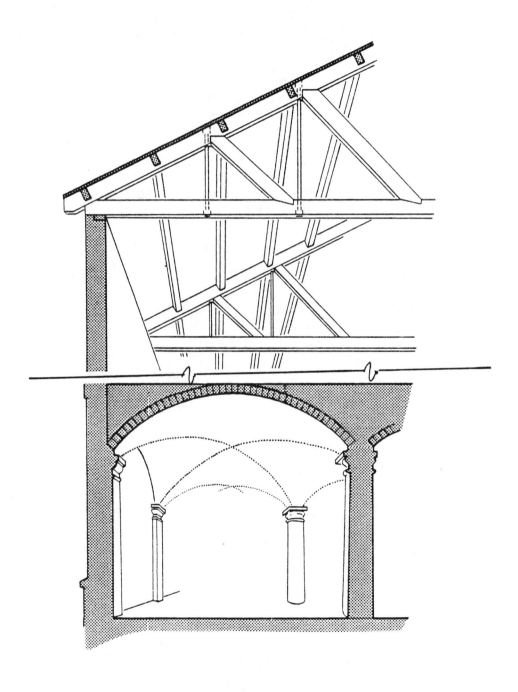

FIGURE 4.1.2
TYPICAL MASONRY VAULT WITH IRON BEAMS AND COLUMNS

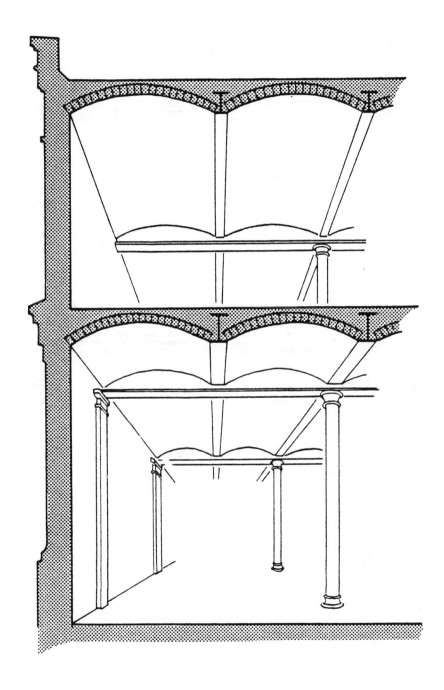

FIGURE 4.1.3
TYPICAL STEEL BEAMS WITH FLAT TILE

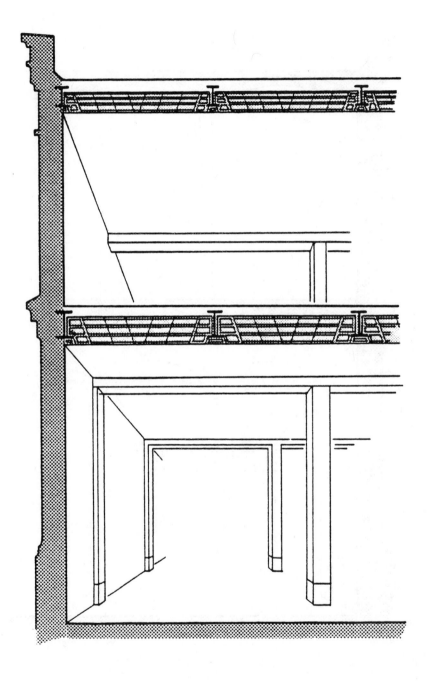

FIGURE 4.1.4
TYPICAL REINFORCED CONCRETE

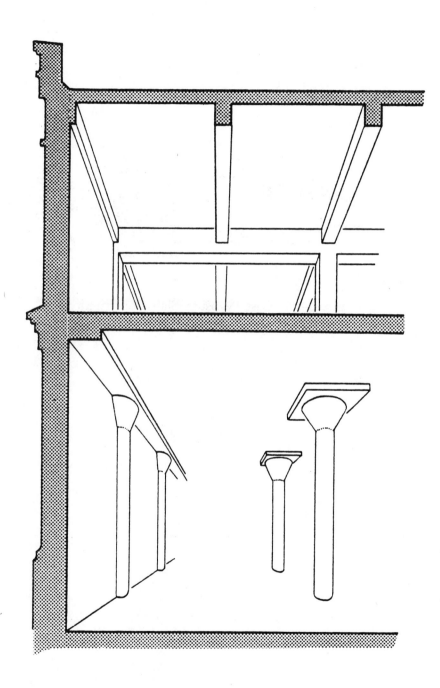

FIGURE 4.1.5
CAST GYPSUM SLAB CONSTRUCTION

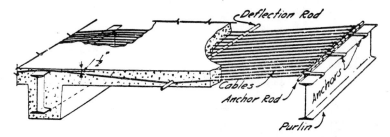

FIG. 6-18. Cast Gypsum Slab Construction.

Note: from *Fireproof Construction* by Walter C. Voss.

FIGURE 4.1.6
CINDER CONCRETE SLAB CONSTRUCTION

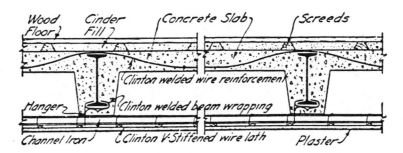

FIG. 6–19. Cinder Concrete Slab Construction.

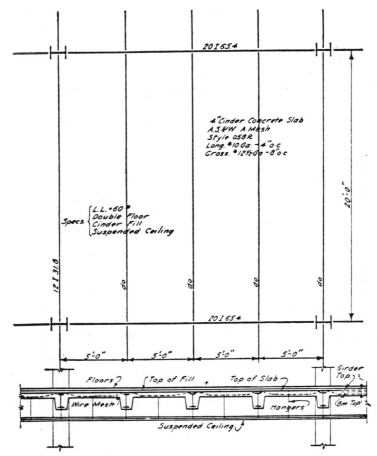

FIG. 5–11. Framing for Cinder Concrete Slab in Steel Frame.

Note: from *Fireproof Construction* by Walter C. Voss.

FIGURE 4.1.7
TYPICAL COMPOSITE SYSTEM

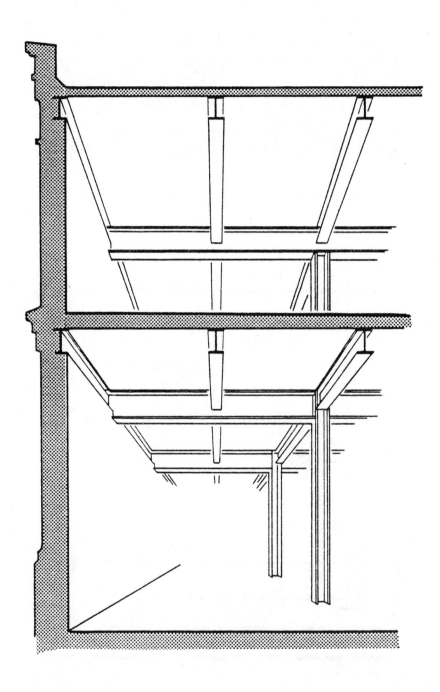

FIGURE 4.1.8
COMPOSITE SYSTEM CONSTRUCTION

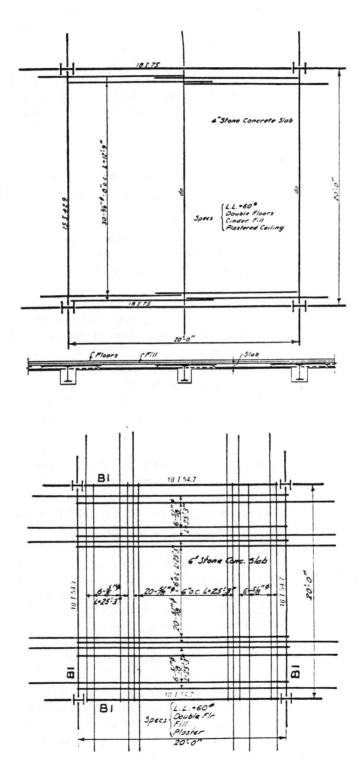

Note: from *Fireproof Construction* by Walter C. Voss.

121

ROOF DECKING

There are two types of roof decks: continuous sheathing, or batten systems. Continuous sheathing is more frequently used today on all types of roofs.

Decking material must be strong (because many roofing materials are quite heavy), nailable, and resist moisture and loosening of the fasteners which secure the roofing to the deck. Historically, continuous sheathing was formed by a series of tightly laid boards (perhaps tongue and groove), and occasionally a nailable concrete deck.

BATTENS

Battens, commonly of wood, are subject to wet rot. They should be of heavy gauge decay-resistant heartwoods and should be pre-treated with preservatives and water repellents. Battens should be laid over loosely draped felt and fixed to the rafters by copper nails, before roof covering is installed.

In sheathed roofs, vertical counterbattens perpendicular to the ridge permit water to drain freely.

SHEATHING

Solid wood sheathing should be of well-seasoned pressure-treated, decay-resistant heartwoods. The wood or plywood should be treated with preservatives, water repellents, insecticides, or fungicides as required. Solid wood sheathing should be laid continuously with tongued-and-grooved, square-edged, or ship-lap joining systems to provide smooth, uniform sufaces. Exterior glue should join sheets of plywood. Before applying roof covering the sheathing must be clean, dry and smooth with no projections.

ROOF FELT

Roofing felt prevents or deters any water coming through the finish roofing from reaching the sheathing or decking. Replacement of deteriorated roofing felt will reduce the incidence of wet rot, and contribute to the watertightness of the roof and the thermal insulation of the building.

Roofing felt should be loosely draped over rafters and lapped sheet over sheet. If roofing felt is pulled tightly, water will collect at the top edge of battens where they abut the felt, and the battens will be affected by wet rot. Battens can be laid over the felt and both should be fixed to the rafters with copper nails. Then the roof covering can be laid.

Following are some frequently encountered roofing problems, and suggested solutions.

SLATE

The thinner the slate the better the quality and the lighter in weight. Slate, if tightly laid and frequently inspected, will require minimal repair and provide great durability. Slate is also fireproof but will disintegrate at high temperatures.

Missing slates, loose fasteners, flaking or blistering slate surfaces, fading color, or excessive breakage, failure of cements or sealants, are common problems. Note evidence of numerous replacement slates or tiles, indicative of past failure; determine if remaining original slates or tiles are still deteriorating.

Atmospheric pollution: The only remedy for extreme decay is eventual replacement with a higher quality slate.

If an entire slate roof is to be replaced, consider the following factors: the selection of a proper and good-quality slate; the structural integrity of the roof frame; the condition of the roof decking, and, the proper application methods. If replacement of roof sheathing boards is required, decay-resistant heartwoods that have been pressure-treated with preservatives should be used. If wet rot is evident, appropriate treatment should be executed.

Rusted Nails: Slate should be renailed with copper nails and sinkers. Galvanized nails may be used if copper nails will not penetrate rafters.

If single slate replacements are being made, holes should be drilled in locations other than those of the replaced slates. These holes should be drilled so that the nail can be driven into the board or batten through the gap dividing the two slates in the row beneath. This will allow minimum intervention while promoting ventilation underneath. The top of each nail can then be covered with a small amount of roofing cement or gasketed to prevent water absorption through the hole.

Inferior materials: Slate should be closely examined to determine if delamination extends the entire length of each slate. Affected slates should be replaced with better quality slate.

Impact splits: Slate cracked by impact should be replaced. Impact is usually caused by walking on a slate, which should be discouraged unless absolutely necessary. If work is to be done on the roof, support staging platforms from chimneys or parapets. For vertical movement on a slate roof, use a ladder lying flat on the sloped surface to spread the weight out and provide a means of support. Horizontal movements will require moving the ladder across the roof or supporting a platform between two such ladders or supports. In no case, should weight ever be concentrated in any one area of a slate roof.

Slates should be stacked on edges, supported by a frame and kept off the ground. They should be stacked in tiers, separated by wooden lath, and should not be stacked more than six tiers high. Cover and protect stored slates and tiles from exposure.

Avoid the common and historic method of making slate roofs watertight by "torching." Mortar is used to fill interstices of slate laps and between slates. This process is not recommended as the mortar tends to absorb moisture, prevent ventilation, and will therefore induce wet rot in battens and rafters.

Note: Other key items of concern when replacing slate roofs are the proper detailing and proper quality materials for flashing and joints when roof abuts parapets, gutters, and chimney stacks. These areas are of prime importance; guard against poor quality materials and workmanship.

CLAY TILES

Problems

Organic growths including mosses, algae, or lichens are particularly damaging to clay products as are acids, metal corrosion and frost damage.

CONCRETE TILES

Problems

Many of the earlier tiles were prone to efflorescence, which should be treated as on masonry and concrete.

COPPER

Problems/Remedies

Problems include: deterioration; folds (copper breaks if deformed by movement or impact); corrosion; inappropriate repair; and thermal movement.

Remedy: Repairs, other than general maintenance, should be executed by experienced and qualified professionals or contractors. Copper should not be patched with bituminous material or soldered. When damaged, copper sheets should be stripped and new copper should be laid in equivalent size sheets. The boarding beneath the copper should be continuous, smooth and in good condition, and covered with a nonbituminous felt which should allow the copper sheets the flexibility of thermal movement. All nails and fixtures should be copper; this applies to gutters and downspouts as well. Minor holes and cracks can be filled with melted copper.

LEAD

Lead roofs may be removed, recast, and relaid but this process takes special knowledge of the material and special handling skills. It is not recommended.

Minor repairs should be made by local burning only and never by soldering. Never use bituminous patches.

The weight of lead to be used for various purposes is important as are the types and kinds of nails, fixtures, and attachments. The pattern of the lead sheets should be properly designed to allow for the roof plan and slope as well as for thermal expansion and contraction in the sheet dimensions and in the joints. Always consult an experienced roofer.

TIN OR TERNE

Lead-coated fasteners and/or copper nails should be used in conjunction with tin or terneplate. Tin or terne roofs should be coated with well-maintained paint coats on both exteior and underside of roofing metal. A linseed oil and iron oxide primer should be applied to the metal both on the exterior and underside, followed by an oil based coat on the exterior.

Cracks

Individual sheets which are cracked may be filled as an interim measure but should eventually be replaced. Cracks should be filled with a non-shrinking caulk or sealant.

ZINC

Problems/Remedy

Zinc is prone to brittle, crusty and pitted splits. Pressure from walking on the roof and corrosion are the source of much failure. Zinc corrodes rapidly when washed with rainwater that has passed over organic material such as lichens, algae or moss, or over acidic woods such as oak, or over copper which causes gavanic corrosion.

Remedy: There is no successful means of patching zinc: in-kind replacement is the only effective repair technique.

GALVANIZED ROOFS

Corrosion is the main problem. When base metal first becomes apparent, the galvanized roof can be painted and its life thus extended. Galvanized roofs which have been painted should be properly maintained. A wash primer, and a zinc dust or zinc oxide primer should be followed by a finish oil coat. Leaks can be sealed with a non-shrinking caulk; breaks require replacement of individual sheets. All fasteners and nails should also be galvanized.

FIGURE 4.2.1
SHINGLE ROOFING SYSTEMS

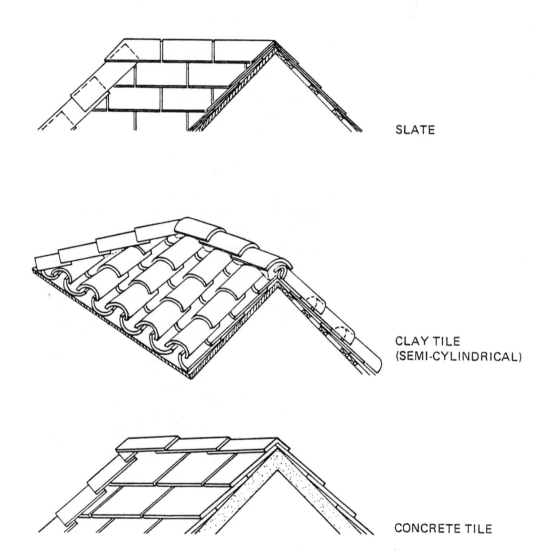

SLATE

CLAY TILE
(SEMI-CYLINDRICAL)

CONCRETE TILE

FIGURE 4.2.2
SHEET ROOFING SYSTEMS

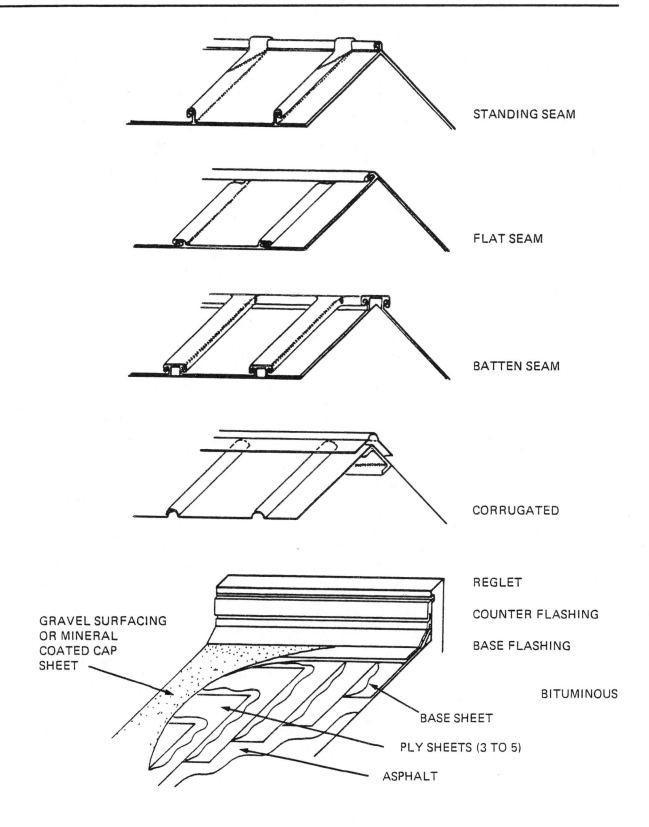

STANDING SEAM

FLAT SEAM

BATTEN SEAM

CORRUGATED

GRAVEL SURFACING
OR MINERAL
COATED CAP
SHEET

REGLET

COUNTER FLASHING

BASE FLASHING

BITUMINOUS

BASE SHEET

PLY SHEETS (3 TO 5)

ASPHALT

GUTTERS AND SCUPPERS

Improperly functioning gutters and scuppers are a common source of water damage and infiltration problems. Common problems include:

Back-up of water and ice under the finish roofing which, uncorrected, can lead to rotting out of the roof structure and leaks into the spaces below.

Washing out of masonry mortar in the area of the leak or overflow spillage which, if uncorrected, causes a progressive deterioration: failure of the weather-tightness of the wall, water penetration into the wall construction itself and related damage to finish spaces.

Staining of the wall face through excess dampness and moisture, leading to the growth of lichens and mosses and the removal of any protective surface treatments or coatings.

Excessive moisture build-up in ground area below the leak or spills area can be absorbed into the basement wall construction and damage interior finishes and equipment. This can occur in areas of heavy rainfall.

Periodic inspection will quickly detect actual or developing problems of this nature. The symptoms are as follows: 1) Peeling paint or stains on wood trim at cornices and eaves; 2) Loose boards or evident rust stains from nails; 3) Stains on the wall face below gutters or in the vicinity of downspouts; 4) Deeply recessed mortar joints in the same areas; 5) Interior water stains on finishes on or near exterior walls with gutters with downspouts.

The maintenance of gutters and downspouts for most buildings is simple and routine: however, it should not be overlooked.

Clogging

Strainers must be in place at all connections between gutters and downspouts to prevent leaves, paper, and other debris from creating a clog in the pipe. The strainer itself must be routinely cleaned. Where leader boxes exist, a screen strainer should be firmly in place to block all smaller debris such as leaves. If torn or loosened, it should be promptly replaced or firmly resecured. Any blockage which does occur in the pipe can be broken free with a long rod. If the blockage cannot be reached directly, disassemble the leader until the point of blockage can be reached.

Corrosion

As an interim measure before repairing of the metal, the inner face of gutters can be coated with a brush-applied waterproof bituminous-based paint. Where deterioration of the metal has not advanced seriously, such a periodic coating can sustain the usable life of the gutter indefinitely. Similar treatment is possible for leader pipe sections if they are removed from the building, but this lengthy and time-consuming process may not compare favorably with the purchase of new pipe sections.

Scuppers

Scuppers, where they exist or can be used, avoid the problems of clogging and deterioration to which gutters and leaders are subject. Since they throw a free stream of water from the roof, they can be used only on landscaped sites where: no pedestrian walkways exist; the pitch of the land is flat enough for the water to spread and be absorbed without forming gulleys; and land is pitched away from the building. The soil content and water table must be adequate for the absorption and dispersal of a concentrated amount of water. Splashblocks of concrete, stone, or beds of rocks must be placed directly under the flow at grade to prevent the force of the water from digging into the soil.

DRAINS AND SEWERS

Where leaders are carried directly down into the building drainage system, cleanouts are normally installed where the horizontal house drain or sewer line picks up the cast iron boot. Where such cleanouts do not exist, they should be installed. The opening, testing and clearing of all pipes where required should be part of the yearly maintenance plan established by the Building Manager. Not only is debris blockage detected and alleviated, but any sign of excessive piping corrosion can often be detected before leakage or interior blockage occurs.

DRYWELLS

If moisture in the area of a drywell begins moving into the building, detected by dampness in the room or by stained finishes, a special inspection should be made to determine the cause. If the problem persists, either the well must be redug, possibly enlarged, and additional depth or gravel provided, or a drain line must be connected to the house drain or sewer.

Following are probable causes and solutions regarding deteriorating metal flashing.

CRACKS

Metal fatigue and erosion can cause cracks at bends in sheet metal work.

Remedy: In general, the entire panel of affected metal work should be removed and replaced in kind. If such removal is not possible, or practical, cut out the section(s) of metal containing cracks, for the full width of the particular metal piece. Replace the removed section with similar metal, joining the edges with the existing undisturbed metal by lock seam; loose sealant-filled seam; or lapping, riveting and soldering, depending on the type of metal and surrounding conditions. Many of the newer alloys will lend themselves to a compatible visual match with existing metals which are required to be replaced. Caution should be taken, however, to ensure that such replacement metals are chemically compatible with any other existing metals which are to remain.

OUTWARD BUCKLING

Buckling in running lengths of sheet metal work can be traced to: a lack of expansion/contraction provisions; wrong gauge; adhesion of asphalt building felt backup to underside of metal, restricting the slip/side movement of the metal; or change of character (twisting, swelling or movement) in wood backing of metal.

Remedy: Using special care, remove the entire length of metal. Verify the condition of the backing material; remove and replace twisted backing. If bituminous felt has been used under the metal, remove such felt and replace with heavy weight rosin-sized sheathing paper. Clean off all bituminous felt matter with solvent before re-using metal.

SPLITTING OF SOLDER AT SEAM

Splitting can be the result of: use of a soft solder on heavy gauge metal; seams not pretinned; high local stress at seams of rigid metal; movement in metal on each side of seam; cracked sealant; sealant age; loss of cohesion from movement in metal; or improper sealant used.

Remedy: If inspection reveals that the problem is confined to one location, remove the length of metal and replace in kind. If deterioration is widespread remove all metal of the particular function and replace with new metal in kind or a substitute metal, as discussed in "Selection of Replacement Metals."

CRACKED SEALANT

Cracks can result from: sealant age; loss of cohesion from movement in metal; or improper sealant for use.

Remedy: Remove existing sealant in its entirety. Use a solvent to ensure complete elimination of all remaining material from metal surfaces. If joint is less than ¼ inch in width, uniformly spread the metal of the joint to permit at least ¼ inch of sealant material. Prime joint surfaces as recommended by the sealant manufacturer. If joint is deeper than 5/8 inch, or otherwise contains no backing material, insert a continuous closed cell polyethelene foam, or butyl rod stock, having a diameter 25 per cent greater than joint width, into the joint. Maintain a distance of 1/4 to 3/8 inch from face of joint to face of backup material. Using either one part acrylic sealant, two-part polytremdyne sealant, or a polysulfide sealant, fill the joint and tool to uniform density. Remove all surplus sealant from faces of metal immediately.

METAL CRUMBLING
AND POWDERING

This deterioration can be caused by: galvanic action corrosion; atmospheric corrosion; erosion; or age wear of galvanized coating.

Remedy: If inspection reveals problem is confined in one location, remove the length of metal and replace in kind. If deterioration is widespread, remove all metal of the particular function and replace with new metal in kind or a substitute metal, as discussed in "Selection of Replacement Metals."

ENCRUSTMENT

This is caused by: oxidation; metal deterioration; or natural patina of metal.

Remedy: If inspection indicates that the surface matter is fairly uniform in color over the entire metal surface, and exhibits a smooth matte finish, it is likely that the encrustment is the patina, acquired by the metal in its weathering process: this will not usually affect the material's performance. Green patina is a characteristic of most copper alloys used until the mid-twentieth century. Recent alloys of copper develop a brown coating. Stainless steel, terne-coated metal, and zinc develop a gray color after aging. Leadcoated copper will age dark gray in color.

PITTING AND CORROSION

Pitting is caused by: enlargement; or settlement of chemical particles from environment. Corrosion is caused by: atmospheric chemical decomposition; or galvanic action.

Remedies: Though the two problems might present different appearances upon inspection, the recommended corrective measures would be similar: replacement of all affected lengths of metal. If the affected metal has been subject to galvanic action, replace all metal in the run with new compatible material.

BLISTER-LIKE MOUNDS

Mounds (with inverted "V" cracks) in running copper work can be caused by: insufficient expansion joints in the running lengths; or gauge of metal too light.

Remedy: Notably, this problem occurs in gutter linings, and inspection should be carefully made before commencing corrective measures. If expansion joints in the metal work are not properly formed or exceed recommended spacing, cut out existing joints, fabricate new expansion joints from like metal, and install in accordance with the procedures set forth in this publication. In addition to expansion joint correction, cut out problem areas for the full width of the metal, and replace with new metal of same gauge, fastening the edges by soldering and riveting.

If inspection reveals that the gauge of the existing metal is less than that recommended for the particular function, size and profiles, completely remove the metal work and replace it with new material of the proper gauge.

FASTENER DETERIORATION

Incompatibility of metal fasteners with base metal is often the reason for deterioration.

Remedy: Remove all fasteners from the metal work, and clean around holes with steel wool, emery cloth or similar light abrasive material, to remove all residue and deteriorated metal. Replace the fasteners with new fasteners of compatible metal and soft neoprene washers to ensure watertightness. In general, use stainless steel fasteners for aluminum and stainless steel metal work; brass and copper fasteners for copper, lead-coated copper, and brass metal work; either stainless steel, brass, or bronze fasteners, for copper clad stainless steel metal work; and galvanized steel or coated steel fasteners for zinc, lead, and galvanized steel work.

If metal around fastener locations has deteriorated to a point where the resilient washers of new fasteners will not ensure a watertight condition, or if the existing holes tear too easily to safely accommodate new fasteners and washers without any possibility of leakage, remove the metal work in its entirety, and replace in-kind or with an acceptable substitute.

SELECTION OF REPLACEMENT METALS

Due to the limited effective lifespan of zinc and galvanized steel used for flashings and water conducting functions, it is generally recommended that these metals be replaced with other materials whenever major problems develop. Selection of replacement metal should be governed by the surrounding existing work and financial feasibility. Appropriate zinc and galvanized steel replacements would include leadcoated copper, AISI type 304 soft stainless steel or, in certain circumstances, color-anodized aluminum. Where replacement metal work will be completely concealed from view, any of the above plus plain copper, and copper-clad stainless steel could be considered. Similarly, in a restoration project, the original appearance of lead metalwork could be maintained by using lead-coated copper, a highly durable modern flashing material.

Gauges for replacement metal should be based on strength, and other performance factors, rather than a gauge-for-gauge selection, and installation procedures should be in accordance with the recommendations of the specific metal producer.

Do not combine dissimilar materials, or install dissimilar metals in areas where water could pass from one to another, creating galvanic action. Use only recommended fasteners to secure metal work.

SPECIAL CAUSES OF CORROSION

In addition to the most common corrosive causes set forth in preceding paragraphs, various metals are vulnerable to corrosion under the following conditions, which should be considered when inspection is made:

a. Oak emits acetic acid in solution and vapor, causing rust in steel and corrosion in lead and copper.

b. Wet woods in general emit acids which cause corrosion in steel and zinc.

c. Fire-retardant treatments and preservatives on wood contain chemicals in heavy concentration that cause corrosion in metals, notably steel.

d. Portland cement in concrete and masonry mortars, and lime will not generally attack ferrous metals, but can be corrosive to lead and zinc.

e. Acid from living substances, such as algae, moss and lichens growing on roof surfaces is corrosive to lead, copper and zinc.

f. Acids contained in cleaning chemicals such as masonry, concrete, and stone cleaners corrode most metals.

INTERIM SOLUTIONS TO LEAKS

Some temporary measures may be taken to stop leaking metal work, but are recommended as emergency interim procedures only, and should not be substituted for more permanent corrective procedures. Temporary measures include:

a. Apply two heavy brush coats of fibrated latex-base roof coating to interior surface of gutters, and over metal surfaces and joints where leakage is suspected, including surfaces which have minor deterioration. Clean these surfaces of loose matter and dirt before coating. This coating is available in basic colors, and selection should be compatible with the character of the building.

b. If leakage is at a joint, trowel plastic cement (fibrated asphalt) into the joint or seams, as applicable.

c. Fiberglass mesh tape may be embedded into either of the above coatings to reinforce the application, particularly if the metal joints have been subject to periodic movement.

CONTROL TEMPERATURES

Emergency Building Temperature Restrictions Regulations, applicable to all non-residential buildings, were published by the United States Department of Energy in 1979.

In general, they require that thermostats be set no lower than 78 degrees Fahrenheit for cooling, no higher than 65 degrees Fahrenheit for heating, and no higher than 105 degrees Fahrenheit for domestic hot water.

Alternative compliance strategies applicable to various systems types have been provided.

Compliance with these regulations requires the completion and filing of an Emergency Building Temperature Restrictions Certificate of Building Compliance.

General

Within these guidelines, rapid changes of temperature or humidity which may be injurious to components of historic structures should be avoided where possible; it is desirable to limit temperature changes to approximately 3 degrees Fahrenheit per hour.

Winter

Due to "thermal storage" in walls and materials, there will usually be a gradual fall to the setback temperature, except on very cold days.

Operating procedures should permit a two-stage night setback (generally limited to 10 degrees) on days when the "effective" temperature (which is actual temperature adjusted by the wind chill factor, as an approximate accounting for infiltration) is 15 degrees Fahrenheit or below.

Morning warmup should also be in two stages: 5 degrees for four hours, then 5 degrees for one hour more (heating system response time is generally on the order of one hour).

Typical operating schedule for a "cold" day would be: 5:00 p.m., building closes, reduce thermostat setting by 5 degrees; 9:00 p.m. reduce 5 degrees more; 3:00 a.m., increase by 5 degrees; 7:00 a.m., increase by 5 degrees to occupied setting; 8:00 a.m., building opens.

Summer

During unoccupied periods it is desirable to operate air conditioning systems one hour in five.

MAINTAIN RELATIVE HUMIDITY

Winter

The level of humidity is not as important as is its stability. To ensure humidity control, have either a permanent or a portable humidifier system which operates in the winter. The permanent system is built into ductwork and controlled by humidstats. Individual humidity control for each room is unnecessary because moisture tends to equalize throughout a building. Portable systems in general do not control humidity as well as central systems, but the portable systems are often more practical for use in existing buildings.

A humidifier system for winter use is required when historic woodwork shows evidence of warping or cracking.

Summer

Humidity control during summer months, if desired, is possible only with central air conditioning systems. In many areas of the country, summertime humidity control is not considered critical because higher summer humidity levels generally are suitable for the maintenance of historic building components, and considerable fluctuation in humidity levels is unlikely.

AVOID CONDENSATION

Condensation on surfaces or within the exterior building structure leads to deterioration of the surface finishes; by running off and being absorbed into adjacent elements, it can produce further damage. Within exterior walls, condensed moisture can cause efflorescence and masonry or wood deterioration. Surface condensation occurs when the surface temperature is less than the dewpoint of the room air. In the winter, this condition is a problem only on surfaces exposed to cold outdoor air, such as sheet-metal fresh air intakes, metal window frames, or single glazing. In the summer, surface condensation is a problem if moist outdoor air, or unconditioned air, is allowed to contact cold surfaces in air conditioned rooms. To prevent this situation: 1) insulate all ductwork connected to louvers; 2) insulate air conditioning ductwork within non-conditioned spaces; 3) pressurize building to minimize infiltration; 4) make sure there are doors between conditioned and unconditioned spaces, and keep them closed; and 5) insulate domestic cold water piping.

PREVENT MECHANICAL EQUIPMENT LEAKS

Leaks most often appear at loose or poorly made connections or in old piping, and they are usually caused by pressure surges in the system or by vibration.

It is recommended that piping slices of all systems over 30 years old be examined for corrosion. Piping systems over 60 years old should be scheduled for replacement as soon as possible. Building operators who attempt to patch/repair 60 year-old piping are running a high risk of upsetting the equilibrium of the old system starting a chain reaction of continual leaks and repairs that, in the long term, is more expensive than a one-time capital cost for overall replacement.

Other than tests and replacement if necessary, the following procedures are recommended to keep piping in good condition:

a. Maintain valves, particularly steam radiator valves, which are operated by tenants. Replace seats and rings every few years.

b. Prevent vibration; install water hammer arrestors where necessary.

c. Maintain traps and air vents on steam systems to avoid condensate fountaining through the vents on system start-up.

d. Install and maintain a water treatment system in order to prevent corrosive elements in the piping system where the mineral content of the water supply is high.

AVOID VIBRATION

Any moving or rotating mechanical equipment will cause vibration if not properly isolated. To ensure that mechanical vibration is not transmitted, the following is necessary at the source of vibration: 1) flexible connections on electric conduit, duct, and pipe; 2) properly selected and installed isolation pads or springs at equipment supports. Companies specializing in vibration isolation equipment can be consulted on specific situations and installations.

INSTALLATION OF MECHANICAL EQUIPMENT

The most important requirement for installation of mechanical equipment in historic buildings is to minimize the destruction of the historic fabric; concealment, often an arduous and expensive task, is of secondary importance. Equipment concealment involves location of adequate space within the structure to house system elements, removal of necessary finishes and sometimes related structural work, and the repair and replacement of finishes. It also frequently involves removal of an existing exposed system, and related patching and repair of finishes. The following information is a guide to possible areas for mechanical concealment depending upon the original structural system and the style of architecture. Figures 5.1.1 through 5.1.5 illustrate typical opportunities for mechanical equipment concealment within historic buildings.

Caution: Every historic building must be carefully examined on an individual basis by an architectural/engineering team to determine the most feasible method of concealment, and the system most readily concealed within each particular building.

LEGEND TO FIGURES 5.1.1 THROUGH 5.1.5
INSTALLATION GUIDELINES FOR MECHANICAL SYSTEMS

Location		**Comments**
1.	Exposed on roof	Only where concealed from normal viewing positions. Protect from elements. Where screens are necessary, pitch them to match original roof surfaces and finish with original roof materials.
2.	Between roof deck and roofing	May be within rigid insulation or furred-out space. Contingent upon concurrent installation of new roofing.
3.	Within roof or ceiling structure	Use only within original suspended or furred ceiling for proper integration within historical context. Reused or newly used attic requires special treatment.
4.	Between structural sub-floor and flooring	May be within non-structural fill or between sleepers.
5a.	Exposed in cellar, bottom floor, and crawl space	Only in service spaces.
5b.	Trenching below building	Depending upon soil and groundwater conditions.
6.	Within walls	In existing furred spaces or new spaces properly integrated within historical context where quality of finishes permits (e.g., as pilasters rather than entire new wall surfaces).
7.	Other	Within furring over structural members; above beam flanges; on top of cornices or other concealed locations.

FIGURE 5.1.1
INSTALLATION GUIDELINES—TYPICAL MASONRY VAULT & COLUMNS, TIMBER TRUSSES

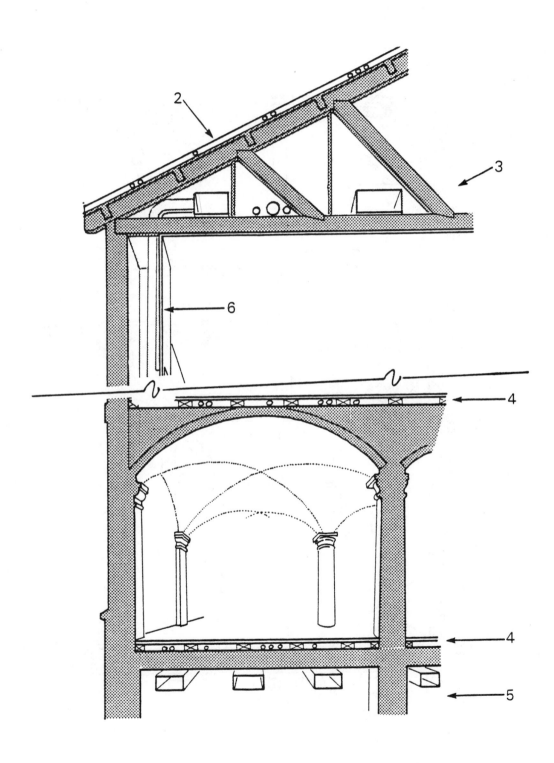

FIGURE 5.1.2
INSTALLATION GUIDELINES—TYPICAL MASONRY VAULT WITH IRON BEAMS & COLUMNS

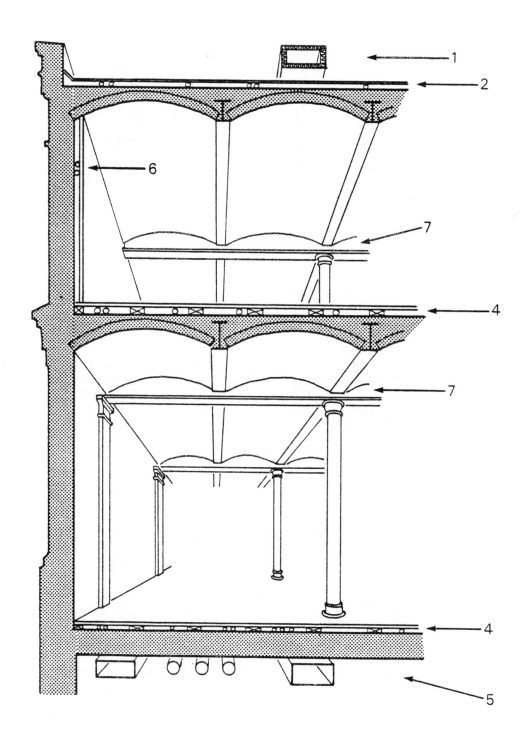

FIGURE 5.1.3
INSTALLATION GUIDELINES—TYPICAL STEEL BEAMS WITH FLAT TILE

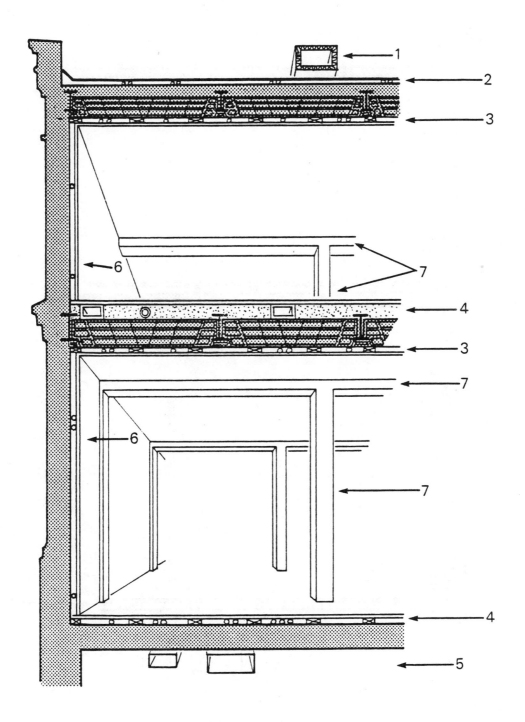

FIGURE 5.1.4
INSTALLATION GUIDELINES—TYPICAL COMPOSITE SYSTEMS

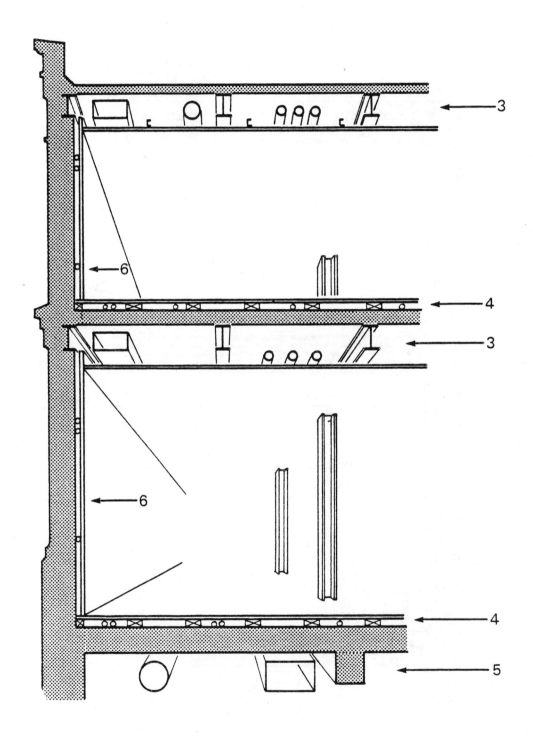

FIGURE 5.1.5
INSTALLATION GUIDELINES—TYPICAL REINFORCED CONCRETE

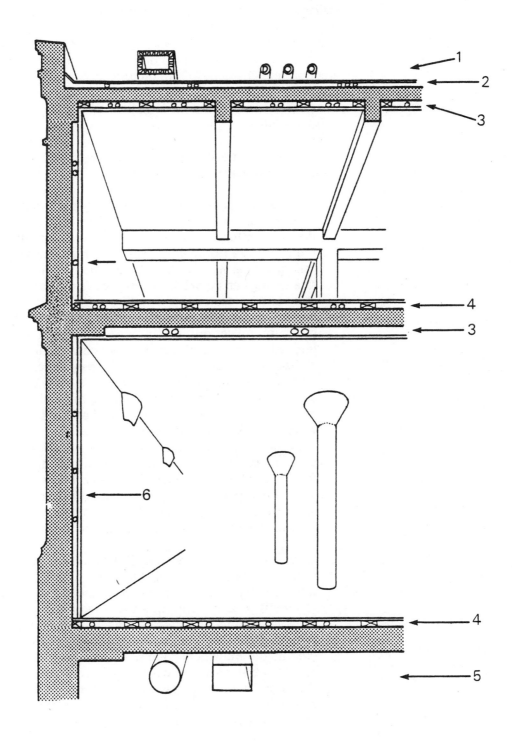

In most historic buildings in which air conditioning has been installed in the past twenty years the equipment is exposed or hidden by a suspended ceiling. Thus, the effort to properly install new systems concealed behind original finishes begins with the removal of existing installations that are incompatible with the architectural character of buildings.

DETAILED RETROFITTING OPTIONS

Some common options for retrofitting HVAC systems in historic buildings follow:

Air Conditioning Methods

On a small to medium size scale, there are three methods that should be considered:

1. **Fan Coil Units** fed from a small chiller and pumps are an excellent area air conditioning solution that avoids the objectionable esthetic problems of window units and eliminates the infiltration problems. Fan coil units can be concealed in ceiling spaces with a 10-inch clearance provided that condensate piping can be properly pitched. With these units, condensate runs in insulated piping to a drain. Horizontal pipe runs must actually be pitched in the direction of return to avoid moisture collection. This procedure is difficult, though not impossible to work out in a concealed installation. The chilled water supply and return pipes present similar problems, but pitch is important only for system drain down. Fan coils must be wired. Water chillers as small as 20 tons are available so this system can be applied on a small scale basis which permits easier equipment concealment.

   If fresh air ventilation is required, a central system which pressurizes the building with minimum conditioned air is preferred to taking in outside air through the window or fan coil units. Pressurization will minimize infiltration of outside air, and will require less power to maintain a given temperature. It also permits controlled filtration of the incoming air.

2. **Direct Expansion Package System** with direct expansion ('dx') refrigeration and a ductwork supply and return network supply and return network can be specified as fixed volume if it serves only one space (e.g., an assembly hall), or variable volume if it serves many rooms. In the variable volume case, special air valves, and possibly diffusers must be used at the individual rooms. This system will be more difficult to install than fan coil units or window units because of the larger ductwork space requirements. Another difficulty with this system, as well as the fan coil system, is locating an unobtrusive site for the condensing unit.

3. **Window Units** are usually objectionable because they disrupt the exterior as well as the interior appearance of the building, and they result in excessive air, dirt, and water infiltration unless carefully installed. However, if no more acceptable result can be achieved with a central HVAC system, window units are an inexpensive way of individually conditioning a room with minimum damage to historic materials. Window units should be limited to the less significant facades. Units are less noticeable if they can be installed in a regular pattern consistent with the architectural design. Whenever possible, installation should be where wall sections are deepest to minimize projection of the unit. Units in windows in recessed parts of the building face will also be less obvious than units in projecting areas of the facade. Window unit condensate drips should be positioned to keep dripping water away from the building materials.

Individual Automatic Temperature Control (Steam and Hot Water Systems)

Installation of individual automatic controls depends on the arrangement of the piping connections to radiators or fin tubes; it is usually not feasible with one pipe steam system because of the shock and water hammer that results when the valve reopens after a closed period. If radiators in different rooms are piped together in series, individual controls cannot be installed unless the system is repiped, and such measures can only be contemplated if substantial alteration or replacement of the existing system is planned.

Where piping permits, the simplest and least expensive method of introducing individual control is to cut self-contained (i.e., integral thermostat and control) control valves into the piping at each radiator. Be sure to calibrate these valves according to the manufacturer's instructions. The second option is to install wall thermostats and an electrically or pneumatically controlled valve at each radiator. This approach would be taken where a central control system existed or where the self-contained valves proved esthetically objectionable. However, concealing the wiring or tubing between the thermostat and the valve can prove difficult and possibly damaging to historic materials.

Forced Air Systems (Individual Control of Ducted Systems)

In cases where conversion to ducted heating systems occurred in the past or where ducted air conditioning systems without individual control have been recently installed, retrofitting "variable air volume" controls is probably the simplest approach. This technique involves changes at the fan, as well as in the individual rooms, with the risk of inducing drafts.

NIGHT SETBACK

Night setback should be anticipated when individual controls are retrofitted. Generally, this requirement can be accomplished by some type of "central" operation, controlled by a selected thermostat. For example, a single selected thermostat should cycle the boiler or air handling unit on and off. It is possible with wall-mounted individual thermostats to incorporate individual (not "central") night setback control. However, it is not practical to incorporate a two-stage setback in this manner, so central systems are preferred for flexibility of operation.

DISTRIBUTION SYSTEMS

Piped Systems

Piping is more easily concealed than ductwork. Built-in vertical ventilation shafts often provide ample space for vertical piping. Design consideration must be given to the location of terminal units of the HVAC system in each room to integrate and minimize their appearance in relation to historic detail. Unit cabinets should be installed either below windows or on adjacent wall surfaces (in which case they should be painted to match the wall color).

Ducted Systems

The size, shape, and placement of air grilles and registers can adversely affect the appearance of a room. In many cases, linear diffusers held to 4, 6 or 8 inches in height extending the length of a room or between pilasters or other decorative features, for example, can be less obtrusive than large square or conventional rectangular registers set into the middle of a wall. Care should be taken to locate wall grilles symmetrically or in a balanced dimensional relationship to such architectural elements as windows and doors. Grille sizes can be substantially reduced by increasing the number of grilles within a particular zone. Careful examination should be made by the design team of the existing space to locate alcoves, niches, and less trafficked areas where new grilles will be less noticeable or out of main sight lines.

Floor grilles are almost always architecturally preferable to wall installations or ceiling installations, since the floor plane is usually darker and below the line of sight, and therefore less noticeable. Although floor outlets are not as mechanically sound as wall outlets, the visual concerns in significant buildings are sometimes overriding.

Old mechanical components (many represent historic milestones) are becoming rare, and their loss to the history of American technology is unfortunate. The following types of equipment are significant.

— Steam drives, possibly disconnected and replaced with electric ones

— Large diameter, low rpm fans

— Cast iron radiators with decorative base manifolds or cover plates. Radiation sections: can be U-bends or capped vertical pipes

— Pipe radiation, constructed from screwed piping

— Pin radiation, cast in blocks with numerous small "pins" to create heating surface and usually found in plenums

— Piston-type pumps

— Slate electric switchboards

— Gas lamps

— Incandescent lamps, with clear blown glass

— Gravity heating chambers, with pipe coils

In most buildings, the original central equipment such as the old boilers and dynamos as well as their original wiring, have been replaced, but occasionally they may be encountered. If old mechanical or electrical components are found in your building, please advise the Regional Historic Preservation Officer. Other interested parties, many of them with local chapters, who may be willing to assist in identifying, documenting, and relocating such components, are:

American Society of Heating, Refrigeration and Air Conditioning/Historic Committee
345 East 47th Street
New York City, NY 10017

American Society of Mechanical Engineers/Historic Committee
345 East 47th Street
New York City, NY 10017

Illumination Engineering Society/Historic Committee
345 East 47th Street
New York City, NY 10017

Society of Industrial Archeology
Room 5020
National Museum of History & Technology
Smithsonian Institute
Washington, D.C. 20560

Smithsonian Institute
Curator of Technology
Washington, D.C. 20560

TOILET FITTINGS

In historic buildings, care should be given to the preservation of early decorative elements, even in toilets, where such decorative items as marble counters and stalls, brass or bronze fittings such as lavatory faucets and handles and stall connectors were commonly used. Such original design elements, when well maintained, are appropriate to the sense of the building's age and character.

GAS LINES

Often gas piping for lighting was left in place when final conversion to electricity was made. This piping or its fittings indicate the location of original lighting fixtures. It may be possible to use this piping as conduit to run electrical wiring for recreation of the original lighting system, without the need for cutting and repairing original finishes.

DISTRIBUTION SYSTEMS

Main Risers, Panels, and Bus Ducts

Often major elements of the electrical distribution system have been installed exposed to avoid the time and expense of concealed installation. Whenever significant portions of the main electrical system are to be altered, consideration should be given to concealing risers and horizontal bus ducts. Often, closets, ventilation shafts, and other small utility spaces are vertically aligned and serve as fine locations for new concealed main risers.

Horizontal distribution can be more difficult to conceal. When concealment, preferably subfloor, is not feasible, distribution ducts usually can be run in the corner formed by the ceiling and wall adjacent to the corridor.

Wiring Circuits

The degree of new wiring concealment in historic buildings can vary with the character of the spaces involved. All wiring should be concealed in significant architectural spaces; concealed wiring is almost always possible in a manner similar to concealed mechanical equipment,

In areas where it is not possible to "fish" new wire or otherwise conceal the distribution, use metallic surface raceway, being careful not to destroy historic surfaces with the raceway attachment. The wiring should minimize its impact on existing detail (e.g., adjacent to a molding rather than across an unornamental surface), and must be painted to match finish surfaces.

Telephone and Other Low Voltage Systems

Inactive telephone lines should be removed. Lines should be run at the intersection of the floor and base molding rather than above or atop the baseboard. Where extensive alterations are contemplated, subfloor ducts could be run along with other necessary mechanical distribution lines, and a new or original finish floor reinstalled for a completely concealed installation. With a subfloor system, adequate outlets can be installed to service a number of desks in each area of a room, thus reducing the amount of visible wiring.

ACOUSTICS, ACOUSTICAL Dealing with the study of sound and sound-related properties of the environment and their effects on human hearing; in architecture, the study of, and design for sound control through the use of various materials that absorb or reflect sound, construction that isolates it, and spatial forms that modulate or direct it to suit particular human uses of space.

ADMIXTURES Chemical additives included in the mixing batch for concrete manufacture or applied to the surface during the curing or setting process of the concrete, which variously accelerate or retard the curing time, provide coloring, waterproofing, sealing, special aggregate finishes, fillers, etc.

ADOBE, ADOBE BRICK A unit masonry material made of natural clays mixed with straw and sun baked until dry; used only in extremely dry climates, as it disintegrates in rain or high moisture conditions.

AGGREGATE Small rock or gravel particles including sand or other selected inert materials which are used as a filler and bonding medium in concrete.

ALLIGATORING Pattern of cracks in paint film which resembles alligator hide and reappears in each new coat of paint added.

ALTERATION The implementation of changes and modifications to existing buildings or parts of buildings in their spatial organization and arrangement, function, character, systems, or materials.

AMERICAN or COMMON BOND Alternates a course of headers with five, six, seven, or eight courses of stretchers.

ANOBIID POWDERPOST BEETLES Commonly known as furniture or death watch beetles: dark brown, less than 3/16-inch long. Their larvae attack well-seasoned hard or soft woods.

ANODIZE An electrolytic process which creates a hard, non-corrosive, oxide film on the surface of a metal, usually aluminum.

ARRIS The sharp edge or ridge formed by two surfaces meeting at a corner.

ASHLAR MASONRY Masonry constructed with large rectangular blocks usually of clay or stone.

ASPHALT A dark cementitious material based on natural oil or petroleum component called bitumen which liquifies when heated and is impervious to water.

BACKFILL	Commonly, soil or crushed stone used to fill the space between excavation or sheeting and the exterior of a structure or around the foundation walls to provide means for water to drain away from a foundation. Historically, rough masonry built behind a facing or between two faces or used as a filler (e.g., brickwork in spaces between structural timbers).
BACK-UP, BACKING (OF A WALL)	Employment of less costly masonry materials and workmanship behind an exterior facing in a brick or stone wall.
BALUSTER	An individual miniature column, post or other form of upright usually square or turned or otherwise decoratively designed, which serves to support a handrail, the whole assembly of which is termed a balustrade.
BALUSTRADE	A railing construction at floor openings, stairs, or roof edges consisting of a handrail supported on balusters, sometimes sitting on a base member which carries the whole railing free of the surface below between large intermediate posts or piers.
BAR JOIST	A prefabricated lightweight steel roof or floor support constructed of top and bottom members made of flat plates, channels or T-sections connected with heavy wire or rod triangulated lacing.
BASEBOARD	A flat projection from an interior wall or partition at the floor, covering the joint between the floor and wall and protecting the wall from kicking, mopping, etc.
BAS-RELIEF	A carving, embossing or casting moderately protruded from the background plane; low relief.
BATTEN	A heavy wood strip nailed across a series of boards to fasten them together. A narrow wood facing strip covering the vertical joint between two boards for weather protection.
BATTEN-SEAM ROOFING	Batten or wooden ribs dividing the roof into small areas and covered by the metal roofing sheets. Unsoldered flat lock-seams providing flexibility necessary for thermal expansion and construction.
BEAM	A heavy horizontal, weight-supporting floor or roof member made of wood, reinforced concrete, or steel and usually supporting lighter, smaller size beams known as joists upon which the floor or roof surface usually rests.
BEARING	The support, or surface of support, upon which a structural load rests such as the surface of a brick wall directly under the end of

a beam set into the wall.

BEDDING PLANE	The surface at which two beds, layers or strata join in stratified rock.
BITUMINOUS	A general term for any material or product in which asphalt is a major ingredient such as black top, roofing tar, mastic, etc.
BLEEDING	The working up of a stain into succeeding coats of paint, causing discoloration in the new paint.
BLISTERING	Small bubbles/boils in surface film.
BLOCKING	Concealed pieces, usually rough lumber, installed behind interior finish construction to provide a solid connection between the structure and the finish surface and providing support for the finish construction.
BOND	In masonry, the systematic pattern produced by the laying of bricks in a single layer or wythe in successive courses in overlapping positions to strengthen the connection of the units, as well as the employment of units that project laterally through the wall into the adjoining layers or wythes to hold the entire wall together. See types: Running, English, Dutch, Flemish, Liverpool, American or Common.
BRACE	Any diagonally set member designed to increase rigidity and/or add support to a structural framing member.
BRACKET	An individual supporting member (usually non-continuous but used in groups) for a projecting architectural element, a roof, floor or shelf, which when concealed may often be solid steel angle and when exposed to view may be carved or decorated, wood or masonry.
BRAZE	To join two pieces of metal by a hard nonferrous filler metal, usually in rod or wire form having a melting temperature of above 800 degrees Fahrenheit.
BRAZED JOINT	A gas- and water-tight metal pipe joint (often called a "sweat joint") formed by brazing; common in copper piping systems.
BREEZE (PAN BREEZE)	Small bits of coke and furnace clinker from the pan beneath a coke oven suitable for use as aggregate in lightweight concrete block.
BRICKBAT	A piece of broken brick.

BRICK VENEER	A non-structural brick wall facing, one brick in width, which is not bonded but mechanically tied, usually with steel connectors of various designs, to the structural wall behind.
BROWN ROT	A condition particularly common to soft woods. Wood so affected eventually turns a dark brown, and in the final stages of decay, it breaks into small rectangular pieces as a result of cracking along its grain.
BUCKLING	The curving out of a portion of a flat surface from the normal line or face under an induced pressure or stress.
BUILDING PAPER	Paper used as interlining, as between wall sheathing and outside wall covering, or between rough and finish flooring.
BUILT-UP	Term indicating an assembly of pieces or layers to complete a product or construction element; commonly used in referring to the flat roof system of alternating layers of felt and tar topped with gravel.
BUILT-UP ROOFING	An outer covering of a comparatively flat roof, consisting of several layers of asphalt or tar-impregnated felt, each layer mopped with hot tar or asphalt liquid as laid and the top layer finished with a protective covering of slag or fine gravel.
BUS	A rigid electric conductor, usually a metal bar, hollow tube, or rod, which forms a connection between electric circuits.
BUS DUCT	A prefabricated conduit which is used to enclose and protect bus running through it.
BUTT or BUTT-HINGE	The common two-plate door hinge, with fixed or removable pivot pins.
CAPILLARY ACTION, CAPILLARITY	The movement of a liquid in the interstices of soil or other porous material, as a result of surface tension; the phenomenon responsible for dry materials sucking moisture above the normal water level.
CARBON BLACK	A synthetic black pigment of nearly pure carbon; used to darken the color of paint and concrete.
CASEIN	A nitrogeneous protein ingredient in milk used in paint (casein paint); acts as an adhesive and binder.
CASEMENT	A type of window assembly in which the sash is hinged on the jamb or side of the window frame and swings either out or in.

CAST GYPSUM SLABS	Made of gypsum plaster mixed with planer or other forms of wood particles, producing light and inexpensive floor with excellent fire resistance and rapid hardening characteristics. The reinforcement used is a mesh or twisted steel strands 2 to 3 inches on center.
CAST IRON	An iron alloy, usually including carbon and silicon. It has a high compressive strength but low tensile strength, and may be cast in a variety of shapes; usually mechanically fastened, although it may be brass-welded.
CATALYST	A substance which accelerates a chemical reaction but appears to remain unchanged itself (e.g., a hardener that accelerates cure of synthetic resin adhesives).
CATENARY	The curve formed by a flexible cord hung between two points of support.
CATFACE	A rough depression, flaw or blemish in a plaster finish coat.
CAVITY WALL	An exterior wall, usually of masonry, consisting of an outer and inner wythe separated by a continuous airspace.
CEMENT MORTAR	A soft mortar made from burning natural cement rock in a kiln to create a powdery substance. It is used in areas where masonry is subjected to considerable moisture and where increased strength is required.
CHAIR RAIL	A horizontal strip, usually of wood, affixed to a wall at a height which prevents the backs of chairs from damaging the wall surface.
CHALKING	Powdering at or just beneath paint surface; result of surface weathering and exposure to sunlight (more rapid with soft paint of linseed oil base). Controlled chalking is an asset as a self-cleaning process that also reduces thickness of coating.
CHECKING	Tiny breaks in surface coat of paint (similar to crows-foot pattern); common to old paint or heavy coatings as a result of reduced elasticity.
CINDER CONCRETE SLABS	Floor system introduced in New York in 1896, using a 3½ inch thick cinder concrete slab spanning 4-6 feet between steel beams. The distinguishing feature is the use of anthracite coal cinder coarse aggregate for the concrete.
CLAMP OR SCOVE KILN	A brick firing kiln, often temporary, constructed with raw bricks and a furnace in the base.

CLAY MORTAR	A soft, low lime mortar usually used when lime was expensive and difficult to procure. Its primary usage was in remote areas and for small scale building.
CLEAT	A strip of wood fastened to a surface to serve as a batten, or as a support for another element such as a row of roofing slate.
CLOSER	A brick of shorter length, laid at corners or near apertures, to maintain the bond pattern.
COFFER	A recessed panel in a flat or vaulted ceiling. Ceilings termed "coffered" are often formed by a two-way grid of beams which create rows of recessed panels or coffers across the full ceiling. Coffers are usually square, rectangular, or octagonal in shape and can vary from shallow to deep recesses. They are usually decorated with molding, often including raised designs in the center. Also, recessed ceiling source of artificial light, often termed a troffer.
COMMON or BUILDING BRICK	Brick that does not meet specific standards due to color, texture or dimension.
COMPRESSIVE STRENGTH	The maximum compressive stress which a material is capable of sustaining.
COMPRESSIVE STRESS	The stress which resists the shortening effect of an external compressive force.
CONCENTRATION CELL	The trapping of oxygen adjacent to certain metals sets up an electrolytic cell.
CONDUIT	A continuous protective sheath for electric wires either flexible or rigid. Also, a plumbing pipe, usually associated with large scale supply or sanitary piping.
CONSOLIDATION	Treatment of the stone surface with a liquid solution which is commonly brush-applied; various stone consolidation processes can extend the life of stone and retard decay processes, but they cannot permanently arrest deterioration. Consolidation techniques employ both organic and inorganic chemicals. Inorganic processes have long life and exhibit similar expansion-contraction behavior as the treated material. Most inorganic processes cannot reattach loose pieces of stone or fill gaps or large cracks; additives may be required for these purposes. Organic processes are based on the use of synthetic resins. Their life span is generally less than that of inorganic materials, but they can be especially effective with porous stones in reducing brittleness and in increasing tensile as well as comprehensive strengths. Epoxy resins, for ex-

ample, are good adhesives and weatherizers, but currently available epoxies are sensitive to ultraviolet rays, will tend to discolor in time and do not weather well. Mixtures and combinations of both organic and inorganic treatments, such as ethyl-silicate, are continually being developed to take advantage of the benefits of both treatments.

CONTOUR SCALING
A crust forming across the surface of sandstones and limestones which follows the contour of the surface rather than the bedding planes of the stones; the result of direct pollution; the pores of the stone are blocked by formations of recrystallized calcium sulphates.

COPING
A protective cap, top or cover of wall, parapet, pilaster, or chimney.

COPPER ROOFING
Sixteen ounces per square foot is the accepted weight for durable roofing. Sheets are approximately 0.0216 inches thick and weigh approximately 125 pounds per square (100 square feet). These roofs are usually applied with the flat-seam, batten-seam, or standing-seam methods.

CORBEL
A stepped configuration formed by the projection of successive horizontal masonry courses.

CORNICE
The uppermost decorative elements of ancient Greek or Roman temple beam sections, known as entablatures. Also, the continuous projecting decorative trim elements at the top of the wall of a room, with simple or complex designs derived from the known ancient temple designs.

CORRUGATED ROOFING
Corrugated sheet metal preformed with grooves, and with fasteners of identical metal and washers to effectively seal penetrations. Rubber and seals provide tight joints at eaves and ridges.

CORROSION
The major type of deterioration of metals; often called oxidation, it is a chemical reaction of pure metal with oxygen or other elements. (See types: pitting, cracking, erosion; galvanic; concentration cell; high temperature corrosion.)

COURSE
A horizontal band of masonry.

COVE LIGHTING
Light sources concealed from below by a projecting cove, cornice, or horizontal recess in the wall near the ceiling, and directed upon a reflecting ceiling.

CRACKING (PAINT)
Large, long breaks through all of the paint film to the substrate

or unpainted surface (on wood, breaks are usually parallel to the grain).

CRACKING (METAL) Cyclic stresses in the metal causing corrosion fatigue which in turn results in corrosion cracking, opening up the protective oxide coating and exposing fresh metal to be acted on by the corrosive agents.

CRAWLING New paint coating which fails to form a continuous film, but separates and collects leaving areas of the undercoat exposed. Causes: combining incompatible paint types (e.g. latex over enamel, oil over silicone water repellents, etc.); excessively thin paint mixture.

CRAZING, CRAZE CRACKS Fine, random cracks or fissures in a network on or under a surface of plaster, cement, mortar, concrete, ceramic coating, or paint film; caused by shrinkage.

CREEP The permanent and continuing dimensional deformation of material under a sustained load, following the initial instantaneous plastic deformation. In structures, particularly concrete, the permanent deflection of structural framing or structural decking resulting from plastic flow under continued stress. In roofing, the permanent elongation or shrinkage of roofing membrane resulting from thermal or moisture changes.

CUPOLA A decorative structure, often square, round or octagonal in plan, rising above a main roof structure, enclosed or open. Open cupolas often housed bells on early public building; enclosed cupolas had windows and often opened to the building below to transmit light into the interior.

CURTAIN WALL A lightweight exterior wall system supporting no more than its own weight, the roof and floors being carried by an independent structural framework. Sometimes used in reference to early 19th century brick buildings but more commonly to mid-20th century metal panel and glass exteriors.

CUSTODIAL CARE Regular and periodic cleaning of building surfaces to remove stains, dirt, and foreign material with the mildest methods and materials that prove effective.

DAMPER A mechanical checking device manually or automatically operated to regulate the flow of air or gases in a chimney, pipe, or duct.

157

DAMP PROOFING	A coating or the application of coatings of coal tar, asphalt or cement bases, usually to foundation walls below grade or ground level to prevent the penetration of water vapor and moisture into the wall structure or the interior space.
DAMP-PROOFING COURSE	A strip or layer of impermeable material which prevents rising damp.
DARBY	A float tool used in plastering to float or level the plaster base coat prior to application of the finish coat.
DECK, DECKING	An unsheltered floor usually of wooden construction. Also, wooden roof substructure of plywood or planking upon which insulation and finish weather roofing is installed.
DEFLECTION	Any displacement in a body from its static position, or from an established direction or plane, as a result of loads acting on it.
DELAMINATION	A failure in a laminated assembly characterized by the separation or loss of adhesion between plies, as in built-up roofing or glue-laminated timber.
DEMOUNTABLE or RELOCATABLE PARTITION	A non-load bearing partition of dry construction, assembled from prefabricated components, which can be removed without demolition and installed at a different location; may be full height (from floor to ceiling) or partial height.
DESCALER	A mechanical device, usually a vibrating needle or blade, used to remove layered surface material (e.g., rust, paint).
DIRT	A generic term for a complex mixture of microscopic building fragments, numerous particles, fibers, oils, occasional organic residue and other materials; its composition may vary widely, depending on factors such as the composition of the building components, its location and use, occupant behavior, etc.
DISTEMPER PAINT	Made with a glutinous medium and producing a flat, water soluble film. It includes both casein and tempera type paints. Distemper paints were used for interior surfaces, generally for decorative work such as graining, marbling, and wall or ceiling paints.
DORMER	A structure projecting from a sloping roof, usually housing a window or ventilating louver.
DOUBLE-HUNG WINDOW	A window having two counterbalanced sashes, each sash sliding vertically in tracks in the jamb or side frame of the window, one in front of the other.

DOWNSPOUT or LEADER	A vertical pipe to conduct water from the eaves gutter to ground or storm sewer connection at ground.
DRY ROT	Decomposition of wood through fungus attack which leaves a brittle texture and partial disintegration of the fiber.
DRY WALL	Descriptive of modern partition construction in which prefabricated gypsum composition board replaces plaster as a finish interior wall surface. Also, a masonry wall, usually rubble stone, laid up without mortar.
DRY WELL	A covered porous pit of open jointed lining or filled with coarse aggregate through which drainage from roofs, basement floors, foundation drain tiles or areaways may seep or leach into the surrounding soil.
DRYWOOD TERMITES	Found in the southern states. They are entirely independent of the soil, and because their holes are plugged, infested wood is difficult to detect visually; technical testing by an expert is necessary to confirm the presence of drywood termites.
DUTCH BOND	Similar to English bond. Joints between stretchers in alternate stretcher courses do not line up vertically, permitting the diagonal cross work often seen in early American brickwork in various localities. Otherwise, stretcher and header courses alternate.
EFFLORESCENCE	A white deposit of salt particles on the exterior face of masonry, particularly brickwork, resulting from the presence of salts in the clay or mortar being washed out of the mortar by water seeping out of the wall during and after heavy rain.
ELECTROLYTE	A substance in which the condition of electricity is accomplished by chemical decomposition.
ENGLISH BOND	Composed of alternate courses of headers and stretchers with the headers centered on the stretchers. Joints between stretchers in each stretcher course line up vertically.
EPOXY	A class of synthetic, thermosetting resins which produce tough, hard, chemical-resistant coatings and excellent adhesives.
EROSION	The corrosion-resistant film of oxide or layers of protective corrosion product are removed by abrasion, exposing fresh metal to the corrosive agents for attack.
EXFOLIATION	Peeling, swelling, or scaling of stone or mineral surfaces in thin layers; caused by chemical or physical weathering or by heat.

EXTRUDE	The process of producing shapes of a constant cross section by forcing hot material through an orifice in a die by means of a pressure ram.
FACE BEDDED, EDGE BEDDED	Stone set so that its laminations are vertical and parallel to the exposed face.
FACE BRICK or STOCK BRICK	A brick of uniform quality.
FELT	As insulation, compacted fibers of various materials in flexible sheet form. As roofing, tar or asphalt impregnated paper, commercially supplied in rolls.
FLASHING	A thin impervious material placed in construction (e.g., in mortar joints and through air spaces in masonry) to prevent water penetration and/or provide water drainage, esp. between a roof and wall, and over exterior door openings and windows.
FLEMISH BOND	Alternates headers and stretchers within each course, with each course arranged so the header is centered over the stretcher immediately beneath.
FLAT-SEAM ROOFING	Flat seams create one continuous roofing surface and are well-suited to shallow pitched roofs and small areas. The sheets are fastened with cleats to the roof surface; one end of the sheet is locked into the adjacent sheet and the other is nailed to the roof sheathing.
FLOAT	A flat tool with a handle on the back, used on cement or plaster surfaces for smoothing or for producing textured surfaces.
FLOAT FINISH	A rather rough concrete or mortar surface texture obtained by finishing with a float; rougher than a trowel finish.
FREEMASON	Masons trained to carve intricate details in stone.
FRESCO, BUON FRESCO	A mural painted into fresh lime plaster; in such work water-based colors unite with the base.
FRIABLE	Easily crumbled or pulverized; easily reduced to powder.
FUNGAL DECAY	Has the following effects on the properties of wood: 1) discoloration (dark or light) in patches or streaks along the grain; 2) loss of strength; 3) loss of weight; 4) change in smell (fungal smell); 5) more rapid water absorption; 6) more rapid ignition but smouldering; 7) more likely to be attacked by wood-boring insects.

FURRING	The separation of finish wall face or surface construction from the main wall behind it, to secure a concealed air space between them or to modify the inner perimeter of a building from the contour of the major structure. Also, the lightweight framing, usually wood or steel, that supports the finish face construction or acts as the separator between it and the main wall structure.
GALLET	A stone chip or spall. Also, to insert stone chips into the joints of rough masonry to reduce the amount of mortar required; to wedge larger stones in position, or to add detail to the appearance.
GALVANIC CORROSION	An electrochemical action which takes place when dissimilar metals are in contact in the presence of an electrolyte, resulting in corrosion.
GALVANIZED IRON OR STEEL	Iron or steel coated by immersion in molten zinc to prevent rusting or other normal deterioration.
GAMBREL ROOF	A roof which has two pitches on each side.
GAUGING	The process of grinding the constituent elements of plaster or stucco.
GIRDER	A heavy-duty horizontal beam, usually supporting secondary beams, often made up of individual elements to sizes larger than standard one-piece construction, such as laminated wood and steel angles and plates bolted or welded together to span larger distances or carry heavier loads than standard beams.
GRAFFITI	A casual remark or depiction drawn on a wall.
GRILLE	A flat grid of bars, rods, punched plates, or other openwork construction, usually decorative, to serve as a screen, or cover which permits passage of air or water through the face.
GROUND JOINT	A closely fitted joint in masonry, usually without mortar. Also, a closely fitted joint between metal surfaces in piping or valves.
GROUNDWATER	Water near the surface of the ground which passes through the subsoil.
GROUNDWATER LEVEL	At a particular site, the level below which the subsoil and rock masses of the earth are fully saturated with water.
GROUT	Concrete mortar with small aggregates and heavy liquid consistency, capable of being poured or pressure packed to fill small

161

interstices, which when used only in small amounts in small areas cures or hardens to normal strength.

GUTTER
A channel for water, usually constructed in paved ground surfaces or at a roof edge where it collects water running off the roof surface.

GYPSUM PLASTER AND STUCCO
Similar to lime plaster. Mixture adds to or replaces lime with gypsum cement (e.g., Keene's cement) producing a harder and more moisture-resistant material; increasingly prevalent after 1930; exclusively utilized today.

HANDMADE BRICK
Wet clay pressed into a mold.

HANGER
A support member, usually lightweight, for hanging horizontal elements such as pipes, gutters, ducts, etc.

HARD-BURNT BRICK
Brick fired at a high temperature, resulting in units of high compressive strength and low water absorption.

HARD MORTARS
Hard mortars, like the units they bond, are strong, inflexible, and rigid because of the performance characteristics of their principal ingredient, cement, chiefly Portland cement. They are characterized by both high compressive and bonding strengths.

HARDWARE
Metal fittings of all kinds permanently incorporated in a building, normally as attachments to doors, windows, drawers, etc., to assist in their operation or movement; hinges, knobs, handles, locks, hooks, catches, etc.

HEADER or BONDER
Brick laid so that smallest face is visible.

HEADER BONDS
Consists of headers only and is readily given to curved or circular work.

HIGH TEMPERATURE CORROSION
At very high temperatures, a kind of dry oxidation occurs, leaving corrosion products on the surface of the metal. If the film of these corrosion products is porous, the corrosion can continue unabated; if non-porous, the film can be highly protective.

HIP RAFTER
A rafter placed at the junction of the inclined planes forming a hipped roof.

HIP ROOF, HIPPED ROOF
A roof which slopes upward from all four sides of a building, requiring a hip rafter at each corner.

HOLLOW WALL
A cavity wall, usually exterior, built in two separate parts, structurally connected as necessary with space between for checking

the passage of water, or for better insulation created by the closed air space.

HONED FINISH A very smooth stone surface, just short of polished.

HYDRATED LIME Calcium hydroxide, or slaked lime, made by the reaction of water with quicklime.

HYDRATION The formation of a compound by combining water with some other substance. In concrete, the chemical reaction between cement and water.

HYDRAULIC LIME Lime containing clay impurities which enable it to set and harden under water.

HYDRAULIC MORTAR Any of various mortars that will set and harden under water.

HYDROLYSIS A chemical process of decomposition involving addition of the elements of water.

IGNEOUS ROCK A class of rock formed by change of the molten material to the solid state; commonly termed granite if coarse-grained.

IMPERVIOUS, IMPERMEABLE Resistant to penetration by or absorption of moisture.

INFRARED That region of the electromagnetic spectrum at wave-lengths immediately above the visible spectrum; the heat in this region of the spectrum which is generated by a visible light source has industrial applications for drying, baking a surface, etc.

INLAY Surface decoration achieved by the insertion of contrasting materials into a surface.

INSULATION A protecting barrier of low conductivity of heat, sound or electricity which limits or reduces their transmission from one element or space to another.

INTRADOS The inner curve or face of an arch or vault.

JAMB The side of the frame of a window or door opening, against which the window sash or door fits when closed.

JOINT The intersection or space between two elements or materials or pieces of construction which are set against, alongside or on top of one another. In masonry construction, the space between adjacent bricks and stones which is filled with mortar to hold bricks or stones together.

JOIST	A horizontally placed member, usually used in parallel rows, in the framing of a floor or ceiling, of wood or lightweight steel construction, which carries or transfers the weight of the floor itself to beams and columns or to bearing walls.
LALLY COLUMN	Trade name for a thin hollow cylinder sometimes filled with concrete after being set in place which is used as a vertical supporting member or column in lightweight or temporary construction.
LEADER	A downspout.
LEADER HEAD	An enlargement or catch basin to receive rainwater from the gutter at the top of a leader.
LEAD-COATED COPPER	Lead-coated copper, which has the appearance of lead, has virtually replaced lead in restoration work, because of its superior durability. The lead protects the copper and prevents it from staining surrounding materials.
LIME MORTAR	A slow hardening mortar made by mixing lime putty and sand.
LIME PLASTER AND STUCCO	A mixture of lime (initially slaked quicklime, later more stable and commercially available hydrated lime), sand, water and other substances (e.g., hair, shells, straw, marble dust, etc.); applied to wood lath or directly to masonry.
LIME WASH/COLD WATER PAINTS	Lime paint on masonry forming a hard, flat, permeable film which permits water vapor to pass through readily. It is economical and, when cured properly, forms a good quality, durable film.
LINEAR DIFFUSER	An air outlet where the ratio of length to width of the outlet usually exceeds 10:1; the width of the outlet usually is not greater than 4 inches.
LINTEL	A horizontal member or beam structurally supported at each end by columns or wall elements and carrying walls.
LIVE LOAD	The moving or movable external load on a structure; includes the weight of furnishings, people, equipment, etc., but does not include wind load.
LIVERPOOL BOND	A variation of English bond consisting of one header course alternating with three courses of stretchers.
MAINTENANCE	Routine, periodic activities and measures intended to arrest or retard decay and deterioration of the architectural fabric, building systems, and materials; involves coating, sealing, repairing, or

otherwise treating these elements to extend their useful life and original appearance.

MARQUETRY
Inlaid pieces of material, such as wood or ivory, fitted together and glued to a common background.

MASONRY
Historically refers to stone or fired clay units usually bonded with mortar. In modern terms includes such items as concrete block.

MASTIC
Any heavy-bodied, dough-like adhesive compound.

MIGRATION
The movement of one material across or through another via capillary action or plastic flow.

MILDEW
Surface mold, often a green-black loose powdery mass; may occur on both interior and exterior surfaces and is evidence of improper ventilation or condensation.

MINERAL SPIRIT
A flammable thinner having a low-aromatic hydrocarbon content obtained in petroleum distillation; widely used in paints and varnishes.

MOLDED BRICKS
Bricks manufactured in unusual or irregular shaped molds; usually ornamental.

MULLION
A vertical member separating and often supporting windows, doors or panels set in series.

MUNSELL SYSTEM
A system of precise identification of the elements of color (hue, chroma and value) by spectographic analysis resulting in the assignment of an exact numerical designation which permits accurate color matching.

MUNTIN
A secondary framing member to hold panes within a window, window wall or glazed door; also called a glazing bar, sash bar, window bar, or division bar; an intermediate vertical member that divides the panels of a door.

MYLAR REPRODUCTION
A photographic process utilizing permanent transparencies of clear, stable polyester film.

NATURAL CEMENT
Lime with a high clay content.

OIL BASED PAINTS	Paint consisting of linseed oil, large quantities of lead and/or zinc white, and coloring pigments.
OLD HOUSE BORER	A ½- to ¾-inch long brown beetle that lays its eggs in checks of well-seasoned wood. Its larvae feed on coniferous wood members.
PANTILE	A roofing tile which has the shape of an S laid on its side.
PARAPET	A wall or top portion of a wall extending above an attached horizontal surface such as a roof, terrace or deck; often used to separate combustible adjoining roof areas or to provide a safety barrier at a roof edge.
PARGE	In masonry construction, a coat of cement mortar on the face of rough masonry, the earth side of foundation and basement walls, or the like; a parge coat.
PARQUET	Inlaid wood flooring, usually set in geometric patterns.
PEELING	Top paint film inadequately bonded with undercoats resulting in partial delamination or detachment of final coat.
PATINA	A thin oxide film which forms on a metal; often multicolored (a greenish brown crust on bronze).
PENDANT	An ornamental or decorative architectural element suspended from above, usually on beams or from ceiling surfaces. In lighting, any fixture hung from the ceiling such as a chandelier or fluorescent downlight.
ph VALUE	A number denoting the degree of acidity or alkalinity; 7 is a neutral value; acidity increases with decreasing values below 7; alkalinity increases with increasing values above 7.
PHENOL	A class of acid organic compounds used in the manufacture of epoxy resins, phenolformaldehyde resins, plasticizers, plastics, and wood preservatives.
PHOTOGRAMMETRY	The use of preset and precalibrated double cameras to produce highly accurate stereoscopic views which, through the use of a complex viewing and drafting machine, can be rendered in exact two dimensional or even three dimensional contourline drawings.
PITCH	The degree of inclination from the horizontal, as of a roof plane or a flight of stairs. Also, coal tar product impervious to water normally used for flat-roof covering and paving which is fluid when heated and can be poured and mopped; solidifies at normal temperatures.

PLASTER	Masonry-like material similar to mortar, composed of the same essential ingredients: clay, lime or gypsum, and sand. It is applied wet, using mason's tools and requiring comparable skills.
PLASTIC FLOW	The deformation of a plastic material beyond recovery resulting in a permanent change in shape.
POINTING	Filling and tooling of joints after the masonry units have been laid.
POINTS	Round or octagonal tools with sharpened ends used in dressing stone.
PORTLAND CEMENT	A combination of clay and calcareous minerals which are calcined and pulverized. It is a highly hydraulic material.
PORTLAND CEMENT MORTAR	The principal mortar material for building construction. For further information regarding Portland cement mortar, consult PBS publication No. 3425.51 for information concerning Guide Specification No. FCGS 4-04100.
POST	Generally an upright supporting member although more typically used with simple square or round undercoated columns or vertical supports, particularly smaller ones as used in fences or railings of wood porches.
POWDER-POST BEETLES	1/8- to 3/16-inch long dark brown or black beetles which attack the sapwood of large-pored well-seasoned wood. Their eggs are laid in wood pores, and the larvae then bore into the wood.
PRESERVATION	The application of measures designed to maintain the original form, materials, and finishes of a structure in an existing physical state by stabilizing the process of deterioration, without major rebuilding, while insuring the continued safety and habitability of the structure.
PRESSED BRICK	A machine-made brick of relatively dry clay formed in a mold under high pressure.
PURLIN	A piece of timber laid horizontally on the principal rafters of a roof to support the common rafters on which the roof covering is laid.
QUOIN	One of the corner stones of a wall when used ornamentally by emphasizing size, or by more formal cutting, more conspicuous jointing or differences in texture or material; also used in reference to similar forms which are copies, in brick or wood construction.

RABBET	A longitudinal channel, groove, or recess cut out of the edge or face of a member; esp. one to receive another member or one to receive a frame inserted in a door or window opening; commonly the recess into which glass is installed in a window sash.
RAKED JOINT	A joint in masonry which has been scraped free of mortar to a shallow depth into the wall to provide space for a finish joint treatment or to form a key for application of a plaster face coating.
RANDOM ASHLAR	Ashlar with units of varying size.
REGLET	A continuous cut made in a masonry parapet or wall face for holding the edge of continuous sheet cap flashing or sheet roofing material which is inserted into the slot and packed in place with grout or sealant.
REINFORCED CONCRETE	A structural system of steel bars or mesh embedded in poured concrete which can be used for both horizontal and vertical structural members.
REINFORCEMENT	Added strengthening. Specifically, the steel bars or wire mesh around which concrete is poured to make a composite structural member.
REINFORCING ROD	Soft steel rod, usually with slight surface projections, used in groups to provide tensional strength or resistance to stretching or pulling forces when properly embedded in a concrete structural member.
REPAIR, MAJOR	The large-scale replacement of worn or deteriorated architectural, structural, mechanical or electrical elements or systems which cannot practically be rehabilitated or restored.
REPAIR, MINOR	Maintenance process dealing with the wearing, weakening and failure of architectural elements by the strengthening, rehabilitation, reconnection or replacement of broken elements.
REPOINTING	The filling and tooling of open joints with new mortar.
RESTORATION	The application of measures to identify and recover or replace the original forms, materials, finishes, and decoration of a space or structure.
RISER	The vertical face closing the space between treads of a stair. Also, a vertical main plumbing pipe or main electrical conduit line, or in general, any vertical run of duct, pipe, conduit.

RETEMPERING	The addition of water and remixing of concrete or mortar which has started to stiffen. Also, the addition of a small amount of water to plaster or mortar as it begins to set; improves spread and workability, but weakens the plaster.
RISING DAMP	Ground water that travels upward through a masonry wall by means of natural capillary action.
ROD	In plastering, a straightedge, usually of wood, for leveling the face of a wall.
ROT	Generally occurs in the temperature range 50 degrees to 100 degrees Fahrenheit and when wood has a moisture content of 30 percent (free water). It is especially common on exteriors of wooden buildings where the wood is near moist soil or in the absence of ventilation (as in a cellar) or in joints, cracks, checks, or splits where liquid water is trapped. The excess moisture content under proper conditions invites decay fungi.
ROTTENSTONE	A soft, friable limestone; in pulverized form, used for polishing soft metal surfaces and wood.
ROUGH MASONS	Masons who dress the rough blocks of stone.
RUBBLE	Broken, untrimmed stone used in masonry construction, sometimes used in simple 19th century buildings as the complete exterior wall; it is more often found in construction of walls below grade or ground line and in back-up construction which is to be faced over with finish material inside and outside.
RUNNING BOND	Modern running bond (or stretcher bond) contains no headers and is usually tied back with metal ties. Modern stretcher bond is usually used in cavity wall construction, as facing of tile walls, or as simple veneer.
RUNNING MOLD	A template shaped to the configuration of a cornice and mounted on a wooden frame; travels sideways along the ceiling line to build up a desired shape as plaster is applied.
RUSTICATION	Stonework of which the face is roughly hacked or picked.
SAND BLASTING	An abrasive cleaning method in which aggregate material is propelled by a stream of air or water.
SCALING	The loosening of a material normally attached to another by surface adherence, which then peels and breaks away. This term is normally applied to paints or other coatings which have lost their bond to the surface to which they were applied.

169

SCREED	Firmly established grade strips or side forms for uncured concrete which will guide the strikeoff in producing the desired plane or shape; also called screed rail; a long, narrow strip of plaster applied at intervals on a surface to be plastered; carefully leveled and trued to act as a guide for plastering to the specified thickness.
SCREEN	A lightweight, nonstructural partition of any construction, often movable, which visually divides or screens one area from another. Also, a small gauge tightly woven wire mesh stretched in a frame about 50 percent open, which prevents insects from entering an otherwise open window or door while allowing the passage of air.
SCUPPER	An opening in a wall or parapet that allows water to drain from a roof.
SEAL	A general term meaning to coat or to cover or to fill a wall, a seam, a crack, etc., with adhering liquid coatings or solid material to prevent penetration of air, water or water vapor.
SEAM	A joint between individual pieces of a material, installed as liquid or solid and attached chemically or mechanically to form one surface; usually a term used with thin sheet coverings such as metals, papers, rubber products, etc.
SEGMENTAL ARCH	A circular arch in which the intrados is less than a semicircle.
SEPIA REPRODUCTION	A diazo process utilizing temporary transparencies of brown-tinted paper.
SETTLEMENT	The compaction of the soil below a building under its weight so that it fails to hold the structure's foundations in place, or uneven failure in compression by members in the structure itself so that the building or parts of the building sag out of level.
SHEAR	A deformation (e.g., in a beam or load-bearing member) in which parallel planes slide relative to each other so as to remain parallel.
SIPHON, SIPHONAGE	The withdrawal of a liquid resulting from suction caused by liquid flow.
SLAKING	Hydration of quicklime.
SLURRY	A mixture of water and finely divided insoluble material such as clay or Portland cement and water.
SOFT MORTARS	Include lime sand mortars, natural cement mortar, and clay mortar and are characterized by low bonding strength, low compres-

sive strength and high absorption.

SOLAR COLLECTOR	A device which collects the sun's rays and transfers the captured radiant energy to another mode, usually heat.
SOLDERING	Sealing a connecting joint or a junction of metallic sheets, piping, and the like by the application of a molten alloy of lead and tin which solidifies to seal the two elements continuously.
SOLDIER	A unit of masonry laid so that the longest side is vertical.
SPALLING	Deterioration characterized by loss of large patches of the surface.
SPANDREL	A vertical surface area generally defined by structural members or fenestration, as between vertically adjacent windows of a multistory building or as below a stair string.
SPLINE	A long thin strip of wood or metal which is inserted in a slot formed by two members, each of which is grooved and butted against the other.
STANDING SEAM ROOFING	Used when there are no exterior roof ribs and when the roof slope is greater than 3 inches per foot. The roofing sheets are fastened to the deck by cleats spaced no further than 12 inches apart and nailed to the roof sheathing or battens at one end and folded into the seam at the other.
STRETCHER	A unit of masonry laid so that the longest side is horizontal.
STRIKING	The finishing of a joint with any of a variety of tools.
STRING or BELT COURSE	Narrow projecting horizontal courses of masonry.
STUCCO	See **PLASTER**.
SUBFLORESCENCE	Deposits of salt which build up behind the masonry surface.
SUBSTRATE	A substratum—that which is laid or spread under a foundation or finish layer.
SUBTERRANEAN TERMITE	Subterranean termites construct tunnels along walls to find wood, their food supply. Joints, cracks, or any spaces provide the best places for these tunnels; these insects require moist soil.
SURFACTANT	A surface active agent added at low concentrations (1 to 2 percent of volume) to chemical cleaners used on masonry surfaces to increase their wetting ability, detergency or penetration.

TAR	A similar product to asphalt (see ASPHALT) although it is obtained as a by-product of coal in making coke rather than from oil.
TASK LIGHTING	An illumination system utilizing fixtures to light specific activities rather than entire spaces (e.g., desk lamps).
TERNE	Metal coated with an alloy of 80 percent lead and 20 percent tin; used chiefly in sheets for finish roofing.
TERRA-COTTA	Low-fired clay, either glazed or unglazed, used primarily in ornamental reliefs.
TERRAZZO	A flooring surface of marble chips in cement grout, poured in place between thin metal strips and then ground and polished to a smooth finish after hardening or setting.
THERMAL DECAY	Decay of wood under the influence of temperature and moisture; manifested in a loss of weight and an increasing loss of dimensional stability.
TIN OR TERNE ROOFING	Tin is generally used as a protective coating for other metals. Tin indicates pure tin coating and terne indicates a lead-tin alloy. These coatings are used today to cover sheet steel and historically coated sheet iron as well. The coating normally is applied to both sides of the protected metal. Both are unit roofing systems and can be used with a batten support system.
TOOTH	In a paint film a fine texture imparted either by pigments or by the abrasives used in sanding; this texture provides a good base for adhesion of a subsequent coat of paint.
TRACK LIGHTING	A flexible illumination system utilizing fixed powered linear track, usually ceiling or wall mounted, and interchangeable fixtures, usually incandescent.
TREAD	The horizontal surface of a stair step upon which one walks.
TUCK POINTING	Joints in masonry are raked out and then filled with mortar applied with a tool.
ULTRA-VIOLET OXIDATION	Erosion of wood, a surface phenomenon that does not alter the strength of the wood, nor its durability to any great extent. This condition is especially noticeable if the wood is unprotected by paint. It will turn the wood brown, in dry conditions, or grey, in humid conditions, depending on the specie.

VAPOR BARRIER (MOISTURE BARRIER)	A material, usually in thin sheet form or combined with a sheathing material, designed to prevent the passage of moisture through a wall or floor with the aim of avoiding condensation within the wall.
VENEER	A thin, nonstructural covering layer of finish material for a wall, as a brick or marble veneer. Also, a thin layer of wood, usually an expensive and decorative species, glued or laminated to a backing panel as a finish face.
VITREOUS	Glasslike, resulting from high-temperature firing.
WAINSCOT	A partial height, continuous paneling, for interior wall surfaces, usually of special decorative materials, such as wood or marble, extending from the floor to a usual height of 3 or more feet.
WATERPROOF COATING	A surface treatment which excludes both liquid water and water vapor.
WATER-REPELLENT COATING	A surface treatment which excludes liquid water but is permeable to water vapor.
WATER TABLE	A projecting course of molded masonry near ground level which may be combined with a damp-proofing system; designed to throw off water.
WEATHERSEAL, WEATHER STRIP	A strip of material applied to the edge of an exterior opening so as to cover or seal the joint to exclude rain, snow, cold air, etc.
WEEP HOLE	A hole for drainage of trapped moisture from within a cavity wall or behind a retaining wall.
WET ROT	Caused by a fungus that attacks wood comparatively wetter than that attacked by dry rot (in excess of 22 percent moisture content). Wet rot has nonvisible microscopic fungal strands, and it usually occurs outdoors where wood is in contact with the moist soil or is frequently wetted by liquid water.
WHITE ROT	A condition particularly common to hardwoods; attacks wood chemically, sometimes covering the entire surface, occasionally appearing in patches. Wood so affected often darkens at first, but eventually it becomes very light in color.
WIND LOAD	The total force exerted by the wind on a structure or part of a structure.

WRINKLING   Condition of surface paint film. Paint is applied too thickly; surface of coat dries more rapidly than inner layer, forming a skin with undried paint underneath.